Physical Development

Chris Heald

Activities based on the Early Learning Goals for under-fives

Ideas for planning, assessment and record-keeping

Photocoymes and songs

Author
Chris Heald

Series consultant
Pauline Kenyon

Editor
Jane Bishop

Assistant editor
Lesley Sudlow

Series designer
Joy White

Designer
Sue Stockbridge

Illustrations
Pat Murray

Cover and photographs
Garry Clarke

Designed using Adobe Pagemaker
Processed by Scholastic Ltd, Leamington Spa

Published by Scholastic Ltd, Villiers House, Clarendon Avenue,
Leamington Spa, Warwickshire CV32 5PR

© 1998 Scholastic Ltd   Text © 1998 Chris Heald
5 6 7 8 9 0   1 2 3 4 5 6 7

New edition - updated to include Early Learning Goals, 2000

With thanks to Military Road Lower School in Northampton and Rainbows End Nursery in Leamington Spa for allowing us to photograph their work with the children.

The publishers gratefully acknowledge permission to reproduce the following copyright material:
Sue Cowling for 'My Day Out' © 1998 Sue Cowling, previously unpublished. **Chris Heald** for 'Christmas', 'What Are You Doing?' and 'Hands and Feet' © 1998 Chris Heald, previously unpublished. **Qualifications and Curriculum Authority** for the use of text from the QCA/DfEE document *Curriculum guidance for the foundation stage* © 2000, Qualifications and Curriculum Authority. **Karen King** for 'The Mud Hole' © 1998 Karen King, previously unpublished. **Johanne Levy** for the musical arrangement for 'Heads, Shoulders, Knees and Toes', 'Wiggley Woo' and 'Five Little Speckled Frogs' and for the words and music for 'Hop, hop, stop' and 'When I Went To The Farm' © 1998 Johanne Levy, previously unpublished. **Tony Mitton** for 'Alphabet actions © 1998 Tony Mitton, previously unpublished. **Judith Nicholls** for 'Clay Days' and 'Making Bread' © 1998, Judith Nicholls, previously unpublished. **The Watts Group** for the use of the text of 'Lucy's Picture' by Nicola Moon © Nicola Moon (Orchard Books). Every effort has been made to trace copyright holders and the publishers apologise for any inadvertent omissions.

British Library Cataloguing-in-Publication Data
A catalogue record for this book is available from the British Library.

ISBN 0-590-53760-1

Contents

Introduction

Physical development is intrinsic in everything young children do. Racing around on toy tractors, organising the play farm or rolling out some play dough are all everyday examples of children's growing physical skills.

Early years settings need to provide a balanced curriculum designed to help children develop their ability to learn, according to QCA's Early Learning Goals. This curriculum should involve learning through play, through practical experiences, through exploration, through discussion and through working individually and with others. All learning experiences should be seen as contributing to the whole of a child's development, and subjects should not be totally taught in isolation. Young children's learning is holistic and uses all and every experience, linking them together to produce new skills or concepts.

Physical development is a vital part of each child's natural development and it should be part of an integrated curriculum for all children, including those with special needs. By encouraging the children to set the table in the role-play corner, you are not just developing personal and social skills, language, and maths, but in the manipulation of the cutlery you are developing physical skills too. In the same way, when doing an activity such as Crocodile river on page 63, you are not just working on physical development but creative development and language too. Children learn much more than we think we are teaching them!

The Early Learning Goals

This book concentrates on the physical development of children along the lines laid down by the Early Learning Goals. The physical development of young children is about small and large motor skills, manipulative skills, physical control, co-ordination and the ability to move in many different ways. It also involves an understanding of the way the body works and how to lead an active and healthy life.

Chapters 4 to 8 provide a variety of activities that cover these essential elements of physical development.

Gross motor skills (Children use arms, legs and bodies to explore space.) They should:
• *Move with confidence, imagination and in safety.* (Chapters 5, 6 and 8)
• *Move with control and co-ordination.* (Chapter 5)
• *Show awareness of space, of themselves and of others.* (Chapter 6)
• *Travel around, under, over and through balancing and climbing equipment.* (Chapter 8)

Fine motor skills (Children develop their dexterity with their hands.) They should:
• *Use a range of small (and large) equipment.* (Chapter 4)
• *Handle tools, objects, construction equipment and malleable materials safely and with increasing control.* (Chapters 4, 5 and 7)

Planning and assessment

In order to be sure that your setting delivers the goals for physical development you need to have a system of planning in place. Inspectors will want to see evidence of planning during their inspections. Further details about the reasons for planning and preparation for inspection are in Chapter 1 of this book.

For the same reasons, you will need to have a system of assessment and record-keeping which is used throughout your setting and then passed on to schools or other agencies who require the information about the children. Further details about assessment and record-keeping are covered in Chapter 3.

Equal opportunities

It is vitally important that all the children within your group have equal access to your facilities irrespective of their gender, race or abilities. Early years practitioners need to ensure that their curriculum policy takes account of equal opportunities issues.

Special needs

Most groups will have some children who have difficulties with learning for one reason or another. Planning is very important for these children since they need

activities matched to their level. Assessment too is a vital tool. Always start with what each child can do, not what he or she cannot do. With special needs children this is particularly important, as they may become aware of their difference from others and become easily disheartened and develop a low self-image as a result. Chapters 1 and 3 of this book give further details on this issue which you may find helpful.

Access for the disabled

Check that your premises are suitable for the disabled, including disabled visitors and parents. Are there ramps instead of steps? Are toilets suitable for use by a child in a wheelchair? Are there provisions for disabled staff? Do your premises allow someone who is profoundly deaf, for instance, to be employed? Is there access to your curriculum for children with cerebral palsy or blindness? Do you provide the equipment needed by such children to support their disability?

Gender

Consider whether there are some resources that are monopolised by either girls or boys. Do your different areas encourage boys to take part in role-play and girls to use the construction materials? Have you checked all books to be sure that they do not depict gender stereotypes with mums in the kitchen and dads washing the car? You can also promote positive images by encouraging both mums and dads to come and help in your group.

Second language learners
Check that you have resources which reflect ethnic diversity. There is a well-proven theory that children respond favourably to what is familiar, while ridiculing anything they find new or strange. It is important that they see people from other cultures in their books and games, or they may react inappropriately when they meet them. Try to include at least one item from another culture in every display, especially in an all-white community.

The learning environment

Encourage children to move independently around the available space at all times. Health and safety considerations must be met of course and children should not be allowed to run around causing disruption to the group. Make sure the children are clear as to what sort of behaviour is acceptable at nursery or pre-school.

There are practical implications in the provision of opportunities for physical development. The learning environment must be safe while allowing children access and the opportunity to develop imagination in their movement. Not all early years settings will have a hall with gymnastic equipment available for use whenever it is needed by the children, and so you may need to be resourceful.

One of the most useful resources is an open space indoors, preferably carpeted, where the children can indulge in rough-and-tumble, use large equipment, dance and move to music, or sit and sing rhymes. If this is not always available, consider clearing a part of your room several times a week to enable it to take place.

Rhymes such as the ones on pages 77 to 80 in this book are another vital tool for the early years specialist. Young children cannot be expected to sit still for any length of time, but they do enjoy singing and making appropriate movements at the same time, and can concentrate for longer periods of time when joining in with action rhymes.

Varied approach
Outdoor play space is also essential for the young child, but be varied in your approaches to its use and do something different each day. You could use hoops, beanbags, balls and so on one day, play ring-games another, have bicycles and scooters another, choose equipment which needs teamwork for another day and finally you could have ropes and swings and slides and tunnels. Alternately, have each type of equipment for a week in rotation, then the next time you use it you can spend some time assessing the children's progress.

Sand and water are two of the most essential malleable materials for early years play, and they are wonderful for developing physical dexterity in pouring,

moulding and using tools. Use sand both wet and dry, and introduce colours and textures to the water, using vegetable dyes, wood shavings or oats.

In addition, all artistic activities such as cutting, sticking, painting, and tearing help develop physical skills in the areas of co-ordination and dexterity.

In fact it is difficult to think of an area of the average early years curriculum which does not contribute to physical development in some way!

Safety

Young children need constant and careful supervision. Be vigilant and try to anticipate hazards – if sand or water is spilled, clean it up immediately; do not allow a child to build a model in an unsafe place, such as behind the door and always keep the room tidy and clean.

Ensure that the materials the children work with are suitable for the age range. Supervise the children closely when they are working with small or sharp objects, and keep them well away from heat sources during cookery activities. When taking the children on an outing check the Local Authority regulations for the correct adult to child ratio. Make sure that you are aware of any allergies, illnesses or other health considerations concerning the children.

Working with parents

Parents and carers are the most important people in a young child's life. In the interests of the development of each child, it is vital that you work closely with parents and carers. The experiences which a child brings from home should complement the experience they have with you at nursery or pre-school. You should aim to provide an integrated system which involves and supports parents in the education of their children as well as their care. Suggestions for involving parents are provided on page 22 and there are suggested 'Links with home' for all the activities in this book.

How to use this book

This book can be used by the adults in any under-fives setting including playgroups, nursery classes and nursery schools, day care centres and family centres. The activities described are suitable for all these groups regardless of facilities or group size, and the resources recommended should all be readily available.

The book is intended to help you plan a balanced programme of physical development for young children. The first three chapters give support to early years practitioners in the areas of planning, child development and assessment and record-keeping.

Chapters 4 to 8 provide a range of practical activities, each chapter based on a separate area of the Early Learning Goals for physical development, to provide short-term planning ideas. It is recommended that you use these to slot into the topics you have planned.

The photocopiable sheets and resources should be used in the same way, to support your planned curriculum.

Other books in this series

There are six other books in this series to help you cover all the essential areas of learning and manage the inspection process. They are:
- Language and Literacy;
- Mathematics;
- Personal and Social Development;
- Knowledge and Understanding of the World;
- Creative Development;
- Ready for Inspection.

chapter one

Planning

To provide a balanced curriculum across all Areas of Learning with suitable ideas to suit your children and your setting requires careful planning. Successful planning will also help your assessment process and can identify gaps in your provision to improve future teaching.

All early years settings need to make decisions about what learning they will offer the children in their care. Whether this is written down or spoken, it is still part of the process we call planning which involves choices of the most appropriate curriculum for the needs of your children. When you plan, there are many things which must be taken into account, such as the ages and abilities of your children, the environment, resources and staffing you have to offer.

Why plan?

As professionals, we need to be seen to be providing what will most benefit all children. There are certain procedures which are essential to the provision of a quality early years curriculum, and planning is one of these. We need to plan for several reasons.

For meaningful learning

Planning is necessary to ensure that learning is meaningful for the children. While children learn in a holistic way and often learn more than you might think you are teaching them, you need to plan to ensure that you are providing what the child needs at any particular stage of development. Planning enables you to deliver a sequence of activities in the way that maximises learning for the children, providing what they need when they need it, and at an appropriate level. Only learning which is meaningful will be absorbed by the children on a long-term basis.

To manage the day

Planning is necessary in order to make professional decisions about the management of the children's day, providing an orderly progression in an established routine. As well as stating what you intend your children to learn, a broad and balanced curriculum will also state how teaching should be done in order to maximise the learning process. Choices can then be made about the approach to be used. For example, if you want to maximise the children's independent learning, then you must provide the infrastructure which enables this to happen, planning the choice of resources to be offered and the way in which these resources will be stored, to fulfil this aim.

In the same way, planning is needed to make informed decisions about methods to be used in delivering the quality early years curriculum. Consider such things as whether adults will be actively involved with the children's play. You have to plan the way in which adults will speak to the children, and decide what outcomes you require to ensure this will happen. Planning is also necessary so that staff members know what resources need to be prepared in advance so that no precious time is wasted.

For continuity and balance

Planning is also necessary to provide continuity, coverage and balance within the early years curriculum. Children's early years should be seen as part of a continuum. Each child will be at a slightly different point on it, and planning the curriculum

should ensure progression for all children according to their abilities. Children should not do exactly the same things in the same way every week. Planning should identify the path of a child's learning from initial contact with a new concept to unconscious competence in its use. It should also ensure that all six areas of the early years curriculum are covered in the right proportions, and that no child misses out on a vital area, or spends too much time on just one area.

For individual needs

Planning is essential to ensure differentiation, and to cater for individual needs. Children learn at different speeds, and so activities must be planned so that the more able children are not held back, while special needs children are not discouraged from having a go. Planning for grouping children in ability levels for part of the day will mean that each child will get what he needs when he needs it, and in a form which he can use. By planning for mixed-ability groups at other times the approach will be balanced overall. Planning is also essential for ensuring that provision is made for equal opportunities in gender and race, as well as for celebrating cultural diversity within an early years setting.

Where you have children of mixed ages working side-by-side it is particularly important to start with the level of expertise of the individual child. Focus on what each child can do and ignore the chronological age of that child. This is important as you may have very able young children, and older children who are slower to learn, as well as those who are achieving at an appropriate level for their age. The needs of each child must be catered for, and so it is probably best to plan for three levels of ability in everything you do. The basic activity you plan should be aimed at the average child in the group, but it should be capable of being used at a more simple level for the younger or less able child, and at a more complex level for the more able of any age. All the activities in this book have suggestions for using them in this way.

To build in time

To make best use of the experiences they have been offered, children need time and opportunity to explore, practise and reinforce what they have learned. Time is a very important element of a child's learning, and a young child will only be confused by being hurried onto the next skill before thoroughly assimilating the first one. Constant practice in a variety of ways which are fun for the child reinforces those shaky areas until they become embedded in the child's awareness of the world. This is one area where planning time in the day for the children to experience free play is absolutely essential. Time to play and try out new skills is one of the most basic requirements of quality early years provision.

To share good practice

Group planning is also one of the best ways of sharing good practice with staff, ensuring that the reasons for doing things in certain ways, based on good practice, are actually understood and become part of the setting's ethos. Professional discussion around the planning for the term or the session can result in new staff receiving the information they need, and can ensure that all staff are aware of the underlying purpose of the selected activities so that the children have the best possible learning experiences provided for them by staff who understand.

The planning cycle

There are three types of planning, long-term, medium-term and short-term. Each serves a different purpose and all are very important.

Long-term planning

Long-term plans provide an overview of all the areas you intend to cover in a year. These plans should relate to your curriculum documents which encapsulate how the six areas are to be approached in your setting. Once you have written long-term plans they will tend to remain very similar each year, and could comprise the topics you intend to cover, and how they will relate to the Early Learning Goals. Long-term plans are essentially very general.

Physical development - 1st term topics

Nursery rhymes (6wks)	Weather (4wks)	Celebrations (3wks)
Large Apparatus –	Wet weather/dry weather	Sewing calendars
Balancing	walk	Christmas decorations
Jumping	Indoor climbing frame –	Controlling cutting and
Ring games	sliding	sticking
Shared wheeled vehicles –	Soft blocks	Tunnel blocks
Carts	Mark-making tools – pencils	Moving to music
Small apparatus –	of different thicknesses and	Malleable materials
Balls, hoops, quoits	colour	Construction
	Cutting and sticking	

2nd term topics

Animals (6 weeks)	Easter and Spring (6 weeks)
Indoors –	Indoors –
Small apparatus such as hoops, beanbags,	Using gym mat
bats and balls	Using hands and feet to take weight.
Manipulative skills with brushes, pens,	Using construction toys for screwing and
feathers, pasta and so on	fastening together
Moving like animals	Outdoors –
Outdoors –	Large climbing frame
Walk around the grounds	Tunnels
Pedalling and steering wheeled vehicles	Tent
Stretching and curling	Parachute

3rd term topics

Out and about (5 weeks)	Growing (5 weeks)	Changes (3 weeks)
Ball skills outside	Linked movements	Left and right turns
Running and jumping	Up and down	Fast and slow movements
Rolling and climbing	Throwing and catching	Trapezes and ropes
Vehicles and roadworks	Stopping and starting	Pouring and whisking
Folding and joining	Malleable materials	Throwing at a target

Medium-term planning

Medium-term plans are a more detailed extension of one area of the long-term plan, and concentrate on one of the topics mentioned in the long-term plan.

A medium-term plan should identify exactly which learning outcomes you mean to cover (in brackets on the grid – right) in the time available including how you mean to assess them and can often be done in the form of a Topic Web. Assessment will need to be planned separately.

Short-term planning

Short-term plans should be written for each week and on an individual activity basis.

As well as specifying the aim of the activity, daily plans should contain the detail of the size of the group, which adults will be involved and what they should do, what the children should do, what resources will be needed and how the group will be managed.

The activities in this book have all been written as daily short-term plans. You will need to relate them to the previous experiences and abilities of your group of children, to the adults available, and to the curriculum documents your setting is working with.

For example with regard to Physical Development and the topic of Wheels, the following statements would relate to activities on page 65 and page 70 in Chapter 8: *Move with control and co-ordination. Show an awareness of space, of themselves and of others. Use a range of (small and) large equipment.*

Opportunistic planning

Sometimes there will be unplanned opportunities for learning which cannot be anticipated or planned for. Look out for opportunities when the children's interest in a particular activity provides a chance to further extend what you had intended them to do and capitalise on this. Make sure this is part of your planning policy and is known to all staff, so that children get the maximum benefit from all the adults who work with them.

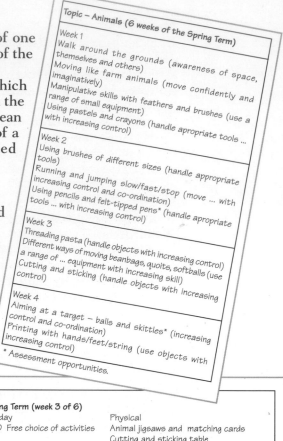

Topic – Animals (6 weeks of the Spring Term)

Week 1
Walk around the grounds (awareness of space, themselves and others)
Moving like farm animals (move confidently and imaginatively)
Manipulative skills with feathers and brushes (use a range of small equipment)
Using pastels and crayons (handle apropriate tools ... with increasing control)

Week 2
Using brushes of different sizes (handle appropriate tools)
Running and jumping slow/fast/stop (move ... with increasing control and co-ordination)
Using pencils and felt-tipped pens* (handle apropriate tools ... with increasing control)

Week 3
Threading pasta (handle objects with increasing control)
Different ways of moving beanbags, quoits, softballs (use a range of ... equipment with increasing skill)
Cutting and sticking (handle objects with increasing control)

Week 4
Aiming at a target – balls and skittles* (increasing control and co-ordination)
Printing with hands/feet/string (use objects with increasing control)

* Assessment opportunities.

Spring Term (week 3 of 6)	
Monday	Physical
9.00 Free choice of activities	Animal jigsaws and matching cards
	Cutting and sticking table
	Threading pasta onto laces (parent helper)
9.30 Circle time	
10.00	Climbing frame
	Throwing and catching hoops, quoits and beanbags (Helen)
10.30	Dancing and singing (Justine)
10.45 Milk and snack time	

Keeping the evidence

In addition to providing planning and implementing the work. it is also important that you keep proper records and evidence of the planning you have made. This is vital for all the staff working with you, for the children's parents and also for the inspection process.

For parents and carers

The parents and carers of your children will want to know what their children are doing when they are with you. Help the communication process by displaying your current medium-term planning sheet where the parents can see it. This will reassure them that you have a purposeful approach to their child's education.

Include some information about the curriculum you plan to use for the children as part of a brochure given to all new parents.

For inspection

Inspectors will look at the planning and content of the curriculum and its contribution to the attainment and progress made by four-year-olds in all six areas of the Early Learning Goals, and this includes Physical Development. (See page 5 for a summary of the requirements.) Evidence of past planning will help prove that your establishment is working along the lines approved by QCA, and will provide written documentation of the quality and range of the education provided by your establishment.

Inspectors will also look closely at the quality of teaching and its contribution to the children's attainment and progress in all of the Early Learning Goals. This does not just apply to qualified staff, since OFSTED define teaching as the interaction of any adult with the children, including parents. As part of this they will judge whether there is effective planning and organisation within your establishment.

Inspectors will consider how staff assess the children's attainment and progress. (See Chapter 3 – Assessment and Record-keeping and also the effectiveness of your partnership with parents and carers. Ideas for promoting parental involvement are given at the end of every activity in this book.)

Supporting your team

Many different people work in each early years setting including teachers, nursery nurses, classroom assistants, parents and volunteers. It is important that your setting welcomes all these adults and ensures that staff are friendly and easily approached. This should not be an implicit requirement, it should be written into a policy and form part of all staff induction.

Time is needed to ensure that the methods and expectations are understood by all adults to ensure a consistency of approach throughout all areas of the setting. You could give volunteers a summary of your curriculum documents, with the essential pointers about how you want adults to behave.

Parents and volunteers in particular may feel some diffidence about the sort of activity they feel they can help with, so it is best to plan to include these helpers in whatever way they feel comfortable. You could plan a leaflet to be given out to new parents asking for volunteers, providing a space for suggestions of areas where support could be given. Not all volunteers will want to work directly with children, but there are always other tasks which need doing such as photocopying or filing evidence or even cleaning and tidying a shelf of resources.

Where planning is concerned, the best thing you can do to support other adults, both qualified and unqualified, is to include them in the planning process in some way. Consultation over planning need not be very time consuming, but all adults need to know what they will be doing, the purpose of the activity and the way in which you want it done. Knowledgeable adults working as part of a team can only enhance the learning opportunities for the children in your care.

Assessment and record-keeping

Staff need to understand the contents of the Early Learning Goals so that they know what it is that they need to be assessing and recording. Observation time needs to be planned so that assessment and recording of what is observed can take place. This time should be built into the week as part of the medium-term plans, and staff should also decide at this point what evidence of children's learning they would expect to see during the activity, so that the assessment can be rigorous and consistent.

Observation forms the largest part of any assessment of a very young child, and there should be notebooks or sheets available so that staff can do this as part of a regular routine. It follows that such notebooks and sheets must be readily and easily accessible to all staff, so clipboards (and attached pencils) hung at intervals around the room would be one way of ensuring this.

Time must also be planned for gathering the information gleaned about each child together in a central record. Consider holding weekly staff meetings to do this as a group.

Put the information obtained by assessment to good use, by using it in the future planning of the learning experiences needed by an individual child. Assessment should therefore form part of the process by which your setting's curriculum is evaluated and improved. Unless assessment is used in this way it is a pointless exercise.

The format of record-keeping should be simple and clear, especially if there are different people filling the records in. Make policy decisions about such things as the language used in filling in assessments, and the resources available to the children as they are assessed. Time must also be made available for discussions with staff about the suitability of the format, and whether any improvements could be made in the process. The children should also be able to record some of their own achievements.

Examples of photocopiable sheets to use in assessing a child's physical development are on pages 73 to 76.

chapter two

Child development

Knowing what an average child of a particular age can do will help you avoid unrealistic expectations and enable you to provide appropriate learning experiences, to extend children's thinking and understanding as well as their physical mobility and dexterity.

New-born babies are totally helpless and can do nothing for themselves. In the majority of cases adults can do everything for themselves, and can look after the needs of others too. The progression from one state to the other is a long and complicated process of maturation, experience and learning, but has a definite progression in which certain skills develop before others, as in the case of crawling coming before walking and babbling coming before talking.

Physical milestones

We are very conscious in the first months of life of the link between physical development and cognitive, or learning development. Many of the first developmental milestones are physical ones such as lifting the head, crawling, standing and so on. Delay in these areas can indicate learning difficulties or serious developmental delay.

In the next few years physical skills will continue to develop but will not be noted with the same sense of urgency. Many parents can tell you to the minute when their child first stood or walked, but few will be able to say exactly when their child first held a pencil in a correct grip, or hopped on one leg for the first time!

In the same way that children will crawl or walk when they have developed the muscles to do so, there are other phases of development which they need to achieve in order to develop other physical skills. Wrist muscles need to be supple to start to make marks on paper with a pencil. Most three- to four-year-olds can make marks on paper which have significance for them, often the 'faces with legs' drawing appropriate for this age-group. or perhaps symbols, letters or numbers which they come across regularly. Many of the songs and finger-rhymes which are

taught to young children are useful for developing the muscles of the hand. Many children of three years-old have difficulty identifying and holding up the correct fingers for a song such as 'Tommy Thumb', being content to hold up the same finger for each part of the song. Very few four-year-old children would continue to do this.

Developmental delay

Normal development is a continuous process, but does not happen at a constant rate, so that a child may not appear to be developing for a while and then will make huge strides within a month. Many children experience developmental delay of this kind at some period in their childhood, but it is most likely to happen to boys, who develop more slowly than girls. Some children will be advanced in some areas and delayed in others, such as the child who is progressing normally in all other areas, but is incontinent at night on a regular basis. Some children are clumsy and have problems with their co-ordination, sometimes because they are impatient and act on impulse and sometimes because they have a poor sense of spatial awareness.

It is particularly important for these children that they receive plenty of support with their physical development, since they are unlikely to achieve the Early Learning Goals in this area on entering compulsory education and could continue to have difficulties for some time.

Holistic learning

Physical skills are important in a child's learning because early learning is not divided into subjects, it is holistic, where everything links together and physical development is just one part of the whole child's education. Young children learn all the time from everything which happens around them, the context in which they learn, the people they work and live with and the values and beliefs which are intrinsic to their environment. This learning at its best can be positive and involve the maximum development and progress on the part of the child.

Where a child is exposed to an environment which is unstimulting, where no importance is placed on him or where there are unrealistic expectations of what he can do, the consequences of this will also have an effect on his development and progress. This may also restrict the child's ability to learn and make progress in the future. There is a strong possibility that this child will be the clumsy or the hyperactive child although genetic factors do also play a part in this. The nature of the society and culture in which a child lives can also have an effect on physical development.

Typical development

Although all children are developing and growing at differing rates, it is possible to provide a basic checklist of what an average child of a certain age may be able to achieve.

Typical physical development by 4 years old

* Is approximately half eventual adult height.
* Can walk up and down stairs using both feet.
* Can hop and jump up and down.
* Can pedal a tricycle.
* Can kick a ball.
* Can build a tower of bricks.
* Can partly dress self.
* Can carry a cup without spilling.
* Can feed self without spilling much.
* Can hold a pencil correctly in a tripod grip.
* Can draw a face with arms and legs.

Typical physical development by 5 years old

* Can jump over a low obstacle.
* Can climb bars and a rope.
* Can sit with legs crossed.
* Can balance on one leg for a short time.
* Can thread beads.
* Can cut with scissors.
* Can write letters including own name.
* Can draw a head and body with arms and legs attached.
* Is independent in toileting.
* Can do a 12 piece jigsaw.

These checklists are by no means the only features of physical development at these ages, but they are a good indication that a child is developing within the normal range. It is important to remember that each child will enter your setting with a range of abilities skills and needs which are unique. Each will have had different experiences to the others in their group and their understanding of the world will be influenced by what they have seen, heard and done. Some of these children will have advanced physical skills, and some will have difficulties with their co-ordination.

Developing skills

Active learning, that is learning by doing, feeling and moving about, is extremely important to the physical, intellectual, emotional and social education of young children. They need plenty of opportunities to be physically active and they will enjoy these experiences. Because they are so young and immature, they will find some actions difficult which are regarded as very simple by adults and older children. Standing on one foot, catching a ball or jumping over an obstacle pose a real challenge to very young children, who will experience an enormous sense of satisfaction and achievement when they succeed for the first time.

Provide opportunities for children to reinforce their skills through practice in order to turn their ability to do something into the ability to do it well. They will also get great pleasure from repeating recently-learned actions over and over again until they are confident and competent in their use. Provide a variety of situations which will extend the range and scope of the children's movement and make them think about different skills they could use in a given situation. Because children have differing abilities in the physical sphere, as in all others, they will achieve skills at different times and with varying degrees of competence.

Encourage children to think about and evaluate their own work, deciding what they did well, and what they need to work harder at.

Space to play

By nature, children aged between three- and five-years-old are physically active, so much so that parents who are not as active, and wish their children were less so, sometimes use the word 'hyperactive' to describe this normal behaviour. Sitting quietly for long periods of time is frustrating for a child of this age, and should not be expected. Instead, they should be given space both outside and indoors to move freely and spontaneously.

Rough and tumble play on a carpeted area should not be discouraged, but should be planned for within the day. This is not to say that young children should be allowed to barge about disrupting play and causing a hazard to the safety of others, there should be intervention from a supportive adult if disruption or safety is an issue, but children need a safe environment in which to practise fine and gross motor skills freely.

A perceptual sense of the space around themselves, others, or an object is not only important for development of gross motor skills like running and jumping, but also for the fine motor skills of cutting and sticking and writing. It is also important in everyday life, and as we are educating children so that they fulfil their maximum potential as adults, this is of great consequence.

chapter three

Assessment and record-keeping

In order to provide the best learning environment for the children in your care you will need to assess and keep records of the development of each individual child. How to observe children at play, what to look for in assessing children and how to keep records are all covered in this chapter.

Observation

Direct observation is the best way of assessing young children. When you observe children at play, their behaviour and the way they interact with others tells you much about each child's skills and learning ability. The child who is quiet and unwilling to speak to familiar adults may be observed speaking freely and without inhibition to other children in the role-play area. You can assess this child as willing to speak to their peer-group at the moment and needing to develop confidence to speak to familiar adults as the next step.

A child who has great difficulty manipulating a pencil on a piece of paper to write numbers may have no difficulty in computing how many cars he has if he has two blue ones and three red ones. In this case he may be assessed as having achieved the Early Learning Goals in terms of conservation of number, but his next step should be plenty of opportunities to develop his manipulative skills.

Underpinning knowledge

In order to assess the children you have to know what to look for in their development. The Early Learning Goals provide guidance about what children should be able to do by the end of the reception year, and therefore what we should be aiming for as the outcomes of a good pre-school education. You may also find Chapter 2 of this book – Child development – a useful aid for assessment. The most important resource that you have are staff who are skilful and who understand where children are on the learning continuum, and where they need to go next.

Observation for assessment does not simply mean watching a child. It also involves expecting the observer to learn more about the child's abilities as a result of what they see. However, observation does play a large part in the way we can assess a child's physical development, since it is all about doing and developing large and small motor skills. It takes a skilled observer who understands the difficulties some children have in this area, in order to assess what a child can do now and then to plan progress in gradual small steps to achieve in the future what is simply impossible at present.

When to observe

To learn as much as possible about how children perform in different circumstances, they should be observed in both free play and structured play activities. This means that the staff working with them will be taking different roles. When children are involved in free play, staff will be supporting, extending and getting involved with learning which has been chosen by the children. Staff working on planned activities will be giving the children new things to think about and explore in a small group. Observation is equally important in both settings, but what is observed will probably range more widely in the free play situation.

Recording observations

There are many ways of recording your observations. One way is to keep a skills checklist closely related to your curriculum and to the Early Learning Goals, shared by all staff, where they can quickly tick and date what a child has done that day. Another is to keep a very simple sheet on clipboards around the room so that staff can quickly scribble down anything that the children do which shows what they have achieved in an activity. Individual staff could also be responsible for the observations of certain children and have their own individual notebooks or record books to fill in.

Children should also be encouraged to think about what they have been successful at, and could have a sheet to colour in or a place where they can stick a sticker when they have reached certain levels of skill.

The assessment process

Assessment is an important and integral part of any good quality early years provision. It is the result of accurate observation and dependent on doing this successfully, but it is a totally useless process unless it is used to inform future planning. The reason assessment is important is that it is the key to a child's future progress. By finding out what a child can do now, we can make a professional decision about the most suitable steps to take next, to produce the best learning and thus the most progress and the greatest benefit to the child. We need to decide what we want to know about the children in our care, and how we are going to find it out.

One of the main tools we have to use in our assessments is the language used by the adult who is assessing. Talking with children and asking open-ended questions sensitively without interrupting the child's thinking is one of the great skills of early years educators and forms the basis of assessment.

Baseline profiling

A National Baseline Assessment has been introduced in order to establish the level of children's skills on entry to compulsory education. In many cases, children have received a great deal of education before they officially start school, while some children have received none. Record-keeping and assessment by early years settings is therefore very important to the receiving teachers who have to complete the Baseline Assessment within seven weeks of the child's starting date at school.

The purpose of Baseline Assessment is to establish the progress which a child makes during the first years of compulsory education which comprise Key Stage One of the National Curriculum by comparing the baseline with the SATs taken in Year 2. Early years settings may wish to conduct their own baseline profiling when a child arrives, noting the skills the child has already acquired before coming to nursery or pre-school. If a further check is made as the child leaves, you will be able to see the progress the child has made, or the 'value added' by your provision.

Purposes of assessment

The reasons why we need to make assessments on children's progress include:
1. To identify appropriate learning behaviour in the young child.
2. To identify any possible Special Needs.
3. To identify the particular personal skills of individual children and share this information with parents and colleagues.
4. To identify the way children learn.
5. To evaluate the appropriateness of the curriculum.
6. To identify the appropriate next Area of Learning and inform future planning.

The first four of these concern collecting information about the child, while the last two are about the action which should be taken as a result of the first four.

Managing assessment

As far as possible, assessment should be part of the everyday routine of your establishment. It should be one of the areas which feature in your planning, so that you know in advance how you will assess your children as a result of any given activity. These assessments should be written down in some form, either by use of a checklist or as part of an individual child's record.

Time needs to be planned into the day so that recording of what is assessed can take place. A systematic process of assessment, which takes place regularly on a planned basis in all areas of the curriculum, is needed if the purposes of assessment are to be fulfilled, and quality education provided.

It is particularly important that a system should be established which can be used by all staff who share the responsibility for the assessment and recording of the achievements of a certain child.

In addition, there are many occasions when opportunities for incidental assessment arise as a result of free play and child initiated activities. These opportunities are invaluable for gaining a picture of the whole child which has perhaps not previously been known to the educators. Examples of photocopiable sheets which could be used in observing and assessing a child's physical development are on pages 73 to 76.

Record-keeping

The format of record-keeping should be simple, clear and easily accessible, especially if there are different people filling the records in at different times.

Keep some evidence of children's work to back up your assessments. Write the date and any comments on what was observed on examples of the children's pictures and writing and keep these in a central file. Photographs of activities and work with construction toys which cannot be stored could also be kept in the same way.

Using the assessment

Having carefully observed and monitored each child's progress within your group and made a definitive assessment, it is important that this information is used effectively.

Passing information on

The children in your setting may transfer to many different schools, or may just transfer to a single one. Whichever is the case, it is important that you have some method of transferring all the valuable information you have about each child.

Where there are several schools, then records could be given to parents to hand over to the new teacher. Enclose a note with the name and address of a contact, and your setting's phone number so that the school can contact you for more information if they wish. Consider visiting the schools if time can be made available.

Where transfer is to a single site, you should definitely try to arrange exchange visits for staff, on a regular basis each year. You could also consider arranging group visits for the children to their future class well in advance of their final transfer, after Easter perhaps. This needs careful liaison between the staff involved in both settings and a certain amount of compromise and understanding on both sides.

Involving parents and carers

For very young children, care and education cannot be separated, one is dependent upon the other. Early years educators need to involve parents in the care and education of the children which takes place on their premises. The experiences of the child in the home should be used to complement the learning which takes place in pre-school groups to help the child feel happy and settled.

You might consider sending home a simple assessment sheet to parents before their child starts coming to nursery, both to find out what the parents think their child can do, and to provide some information about what will be expected of their child in your group.

chapter four

Manipulative skills

Children need to develop their dexterity in order to be able to draw and write. Time to practise new skills is essential and a variety of different approaches are needed to keep the children's interest. In this chapter a range of new activities provide suggestions for developing manipulative skills.

Matching shoes

Learning outcome

To move everyday objects to make pairs. To attempt to fasten laces.

Group size

Eight to ten children.

What you need

Pairs of shoes in different colours; ensure at least one of the pairs has laces (try jumble sales for shoes and wipe them with a mild disinfectant before use), the chorus of the song *Blue suede shoes* sung with different colours. Photocopiable sheet on page 88.

Preparation

Mix all the shoes together in a heap on the floor. Provide a photocopiable sheet for each child.

What to do

Look at the pile of shoes together and ask each of the children in turn to say a colour that they can see in the pile of shoes. Sing the chorus of *Blue suede shoes* for the named colour while the child searches for a pair of shoes of that colour.

Young children frequently mix up the names of their colours, so if a child ends up with a different coloured pair of shoes from the named one, just say 'Oh, you've got *green* shoes', and sing the song again for the correct colour! Gradually put the shoes together in pairs until they are all sorted.

Talk about the similarities and differences between all the shoes.

Encourage each child to have a go at fastening the laces on one of the shoes.

Finally give each child a photocopiable sheet and ask them to colour the pairs of shoes in three matching colours.

Questions to ask

What shoes have you got at home? Who wears big shoes in your house? What shoes would you wear if it was raining? What would you do if you were wearing these shoes?

For younger children

The physical matching of the shoes is sufficient for younger children, as recording is not always appropriate for them. They may find attempting to tie the laces very frustrating.

For older children

Older children could cut out the shoes on the sheet and stick them together in pairs in a workbook.

Follow-up activities

* Say the poem 'What are you doing?' on page 78.
* Choose a colour theme in the role-play area and provide the children with shoes, dresses and hats in that colour.
* Colour the sand and water in the colour of the week.

Links with home

Ask parents to bring in any clean, brightly-coloured shoes they no longer use.

Tools galore!

Learning outcome

To choose an appropriate tool for a task.

Group size

Four children.

What you need

Sheets of A4 paper, thick and thin sponge brushes, fine brushes (size 4), thick brushes (size 12), rollers of various widths, twigs, scrapers, felt-tipped pens, pencils and crayons (thick and fine), containers for storage (one for each different type of tool), paint in assorted colours, PVA glue, A3 paper, 10cm squares of watercolour paper (available from stockists of artists' materials), a container of flowers of different sizes and shapes together with some attractive leaves.

Preparation

Label the containers clearly with their contents and ensure that the containers are easily accessible to the children. Make sure that the children can choose which tools they are going to use.

What to do

Invite the children to look at the flowers and leaves you have provided. Ask them to each select one flower and to hold it carefully. Encourage them to look inside it and to tell you what they can see. Point out the shapes of the leaves and the different shades of green which can be seen.

When the children have had plenty of time to look at, touch and smell the flowers, ask them to choose either a large or a small piece of paper to paint

a picture. Explain that they will all be doing two pictures so that they can choose which size they do first.

Next ask the children to choose the tools they want to use for their pictures. Encourage them to look carefully at the flowers and leaves while they paint. After their first attempts ask the children to try another flower or leaf on a different-sized piece of paper.

Encourage the children to consider all the available tools and to select which they think the best for the job.

Questions to ask

What sort of mark will that brush make? What flower are you going to paint? Is it going to be a large or small flower? What paper are you going to use? Why did you choose that? What are you going to do next? Why did that happen? How could you change it, if you did it again?

For younger children

With younger children select one variety of flower at a time (such as a daffodil), and restrict the colour choices to shades of yellow and green.

For older children

Older children might enjoy looking at famous flower paintings, such as Van Gogh's *Sunflowers* and *Irises*, Monet's *Waterlilies*, sixteenth-century Dutch flower paintings, or more modern artists' work such as Georgia O'Keeffe.

Links with home

Ask a parent who is a D.I.Y enthusiast or one who is a chef to come and show some tools to the children and talk about the need to have the right tool for the right job.

Follow-up activities

∗ Use small flower pictures on watercolour paper for Mother's Day cards, mounting them onto a larger piece of card.
∗ Start a sketch-book for each child, where they can keep their favourite drawings.
∗ Ask the children to sort out the tools in the work-area into a set of tools which can be used for large paintings, and a set of tools which can be used for small paintings.

Feather patterns

To develop increasing manual control of objects.

Group size
Four children.

What you need
Sturdy feathers with a firm spine (such as those from a bird's wing or tail). Thin paint or washable ink of various colours, a plastic palette, sheets of paper, a sharp craft knife (to be used by an adult only).

Preparation
Put the paint or ink into the plastic palette. The feathers will need to be washed carefully in a mild disinfectant solution. Be aware of any children who may be allergic to feathers. Prepare enough quills for the children in advance. Cut sharp points on some of the feathers, then cut across at the top to form a nib (see below).

step 1 step 2

What to do
Talk about the feathers with the children and establish if they know what they are, and where they come from. Warn them not to put the feathers near their noses or mouths. Ask them if they think they can use the feathers to do anything, and after they have finished tickling each other with them, explain that you are going to show them how to use the feathers to write (make marks). Show the children how you have cut the end of the quill of the feather and demonstrate how it can be used as a pen to make patterns and swirls when dipped into the paint or ink.

Encourage the children to experiment with using the quills, and see if they can write all or part of their own name. Ask them if they can think of any other ways they could use a feather to make marks.

Rook's Feathers

Questions to ask
Where do you think we get feathers from? What are they used for? What do birds use them for? What can you do with this feather? How could we make marks with it? Which end should we use first? Are there any other things you could do with this feather?

For younger children
With younger children, concentrate on using the feather to make swirls and patterns on the paper rather than actually writing with it.

For older children
Older children could do some work on the history of writing, attempting to copy some of the elaborate scrolling on signatures from the past, such as Elizabeth I.

Follow-up activities
∗ Experiment with different types of feathers to find the best ones to use for writing and making patterns.
∗ Display some feathers next to a picture of the bird they came from and show examples of the marks it can make.
∗ Pick up leaves and pieces of twig and use them to make patterns with paint or ink.

Links with home
If any of your parents keep birds as pets, arrange for them to bring them in; this would be a good start to the activity, and a reliable source of feathers! Other parents may be knowledgeable about the wild birds in your area.

String printing

Learning outcome

To handle appropriate tools and objects.

Group size
Six children.

What you need
Shallow trays for holding paint, fairly coarse jute string, large paintbrushes (size 12), a choice of paints, complementary or contrasting coloured A3-sized paper (a combination of gold and black or red and yellow is effective), scissors.

Preparation
Help the children to cut the string into approximately 40cm lengths and pour the paint into the trays. Ask the children to fold the paper more-or-less in half.

What to do
Demonstrate to the children what you want them to do. Show them how to drop a piece of string into the tray and to use the paintbrush to ensure it is covered in paint. Lift the string onto one half of the pre-folded paper and arrange it into a pattern, with one end hanging out. Fold the paper over the string and press down, pulling the string out to make shell-like fluted patterns.

Encourage the children to each make their own pattern. If they can't manage to press down on the paper while they pull, you could perhaps help them to do this.

Questions to ask
How long do you want to make that string? Which colour do you want to use? Why? What are you going to do next? Where are you going to put the paint? What pattern have you made? What was easy about making your pattern? What was hard?

For younger children
Younger children might find it easier to press the paper with a rolling-pin and pull the string out afterwards.

For older children
Older children could make a second pattern in a different colour on top of the first one, arranging the string to fill the spaces left.

Follow-up activities
∗ Encourage the children to practise tying knots or bows in the different coloured strings and use them for threading beads and so on.
∗ Glue string to pieces of wood to use for block-printing.
∗ Make letter-shapes from string and glue them to card so that the children can run their fingers over them to appreciate their shape.

Links with home

Prepare a short note explaining what the children have done, and what skills they have developed. Send this home with the child's print.

Tearing tissue

Learning outcome

To handle appropriate materials with increasing control.

Group size

Six children.

What you need.

Tissue paper in a large variety of shades of colours, PVA glue, glue pots, water, thick paint brushes (size 12), white paper (A4).

Preparation

Mix the PVA glue with equal amounts of water, to provide a thin runny glue.

What to do

Take the children to look at some trees. Whatever time of year it is there should be plenty to see. In spring, they can look at blossom and the shapes this makes against the new pale green foliage. In summer, they can look at the different shades of green in each patch of foliage, while in autumn they can look at the glowing colours of the dying leaves. Ask the children to look carefully at the shape of the tree, regardless of the season. Point out the trunk which holds up all the branches and leaves.

When you return to your base, ask each child to choose a piece of tissue and to tear it into the shape of the trunk of the tree. Encourage the children to place their torn piece of tissue on their sheet of paper where they want the trunk of their tree to be, and then paint on top of it with the glue solution. As the tissue is very thin, this will stick it firmly to the paper.

The children can now start to tear pieces of tissue to represent the foliage of the tree, overlapping different shades to form blocks of appropriate colour for the time of year, and continuing to paint over with the glue. The torn edges of the tissue make an attractive random effect for the foliage, and the children can arrange the tissue as they wish before painting over the top to fix it in place.

Questions to ask

What time of year is it now? What do the trees look like? Why? What sort of trees do you like? Where can you see lots of trees? What colours are you going to put on your tree? Why have you put the trunk there?

For younger children

Offer younger children a limited range of colours, for example yellow and blue, and let them experiment with producing different shades by overlaying their torn pieces.

For older children

Older children can draw on top of a torn-tissue picture with felt-tipped pens to add detail.

Follow-up activities

* Use other forms of paper, including sweet-wrappings and wallpaper for torn-paper collage.
* Make tissue name-cards by tearing pieces of tissue and sticking them together to form letters on a strip of card.
* Use photocopiable page 89 and ask the children to use their tearing skills to put the picture together.
* Say the rhyme 'Alphabet actions' on page 80.

Links with home

Put up a notice telling parents that the children have been making pictures using torn paper and asking if any parent has access to free supplies.

Blown away!

Learning outcome

To handle appropriate tools with increasing control.

Group size

Four children.

What you need

A4 paper or card, ink or paint in contrasting colours in plastic beakers, plastic drinking straws which are longer than the height of the beakers.

Preparation

Cover your surfaces with a protective layer of some kind, as the paint is liable to travel over the edge of the paper. Make sure that the ink or paint is thin enough to move easily when blown.

What to do

Practise blowing through the straw with your group. Some young children will find this difficult; make sure they don't suck instead!

Show the children how to lift paint with a straw by putting your finger over the top when the straw is in the beaker Show them what happens to the paint when you take your finger off the straw.

Ask the children if they can make a puddle of paint on their page using the straws. Ask them what they think will happen if you blow the paint with your straw.

Demonstrate how you can get the paint to snake in tendrils across the paper. Point out that you can choose where to send the paint. Encourage each child to experiment and see what they can do with the paint.

Questions to ask

What do you think will happen if I put my finger over the top of the straw? What will happen if I take my finger off? What are you going to use to make your picture? What has happened to your paint now? Where are you going to send it next? Can you blow the paint in a straight/wiggly line?

For younger children

Younger children will not be able to use straws to pick up paint so let them try using droppers or drips from a wet paintbrush to make their puddle. They could still experiment with blowing the paint with the straws in the same way.

For older children

Suggest that older children could consider using several colours on one picture. They could also try to make their picture represent an object or scene rather than a random pattern.

Follow-up activities

* Provide small sailing boats and straws in the water tray. Let the children have a race to see which boat can reach the far side first.
* Stand a rigid plastic straw upright in a lump of Plasticine use it for threading beads in a vertical instead of a horizontal way.

Links with home

Ask parents and children to each bring in a straw from home. Look at the straws and encourage the children to sort them for similarities and differences.

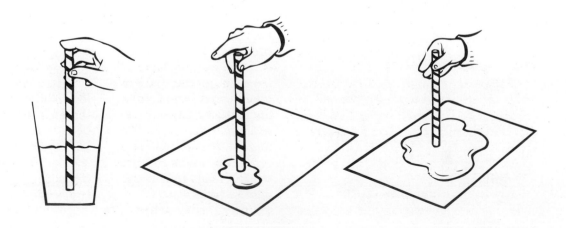

Take a letter

To handle appropriate tools and objects safely and with increasing control.

Group size
Eight children.

What you need
Large sheets of paper (A3), assorted felt-tipped pens.

Preparation
Pour glue into containers. Put collage materials so that they are easily accessible for the children. Decide in advance which letter your group will concentrate on. Letters can be divided into groups of similarly formed letters, such as n, m, h, and r; or c, a, d, and q, and it is better to tackle each 'family' of letters together, perhaps over the course of a week.

What to do
Draw a large outline of your chosen letter onto a sheet of paper while explaining to the children what arm movements you are making; up, down, round and so on.

Then ask the children to choose a felt-tipped pen and make a big outline of the letter on their own sheet of paper. Ask them to go over this several times, using different colours, so that they end up with a thick rainbow-coloured letter. Talk to the children about the shape of this letter, and what sound it makes. Repeat the activity using other letters.

Questions to ask
What sound does this letter make? What words begin with this sound? Why did you choose that colour? What does it look like? What are you going to do now? What shapes can you make with your arm?

For younger children
Do not expect younger children to copy letters, but let them experiment by making marks on their paper in several different colours using large arm movements.

For older children
Older children could design a figure using the shape of the letter and adding faces, feet and hands.

Follow-up activities
* Invite the children to stick collage materials on their letter, following the outline in the same way as they drew it .
* Make an alphabet frieze using the children's own designs and display the letters in the correct order.
* Encourage children to paint the letters in their name using thin paint, going over it lots of times with different colours or shades of colour.

Links with home
Suggest that parents buy a set of the magnetic letters which can be used on the doors of fridges, and let their child handle them and make words with them.

Whisking it up

Learning outcome

To gain control in manipulating tools.

Group size

Four children.

What you need

Hand and rotary whisks, wooden spoons, mild shampoo or bubble bath, a water-tray or large unbreakable bowl, smaller plastic bowls or containers, aprons, plastic magnifying glasses.

Preparation

Make sure the rotary whisks are smooth and easy to operate, oiling them with a little vegetable oil if necessary. Pour shampoo or bubble bath into the water. Remember to check for allergies to soap products.

What to do

Show the children how the soapy water will froth up when it is beaten with hands, the whisks or a wooden spoon. Ask them to put on the aprons and let them experiment themselves. Tell the children to listen very carefully to the noise the frothy bubbles make when they burst.

Scoop up the froth with the small bowls and make pies with it, or pile it up into mountains. Place some froth on a table top, and encourage the children to look closely at it using the magnifying glasses.

Questions to ask

How can you make more bubbles? What can you hear? How do the bubbles feel when you touch them? Where do you have bubbles like this at home? What else is white like this froth? What can you see when you look through the magnifying glass?

For younger children

Younger children will find difficulty using whisks and should start by experimenting with their hands. Once they have had plenty of experience with their hands, introduce the whisks and wooden spoons and be there to help them if necessary.

For older children

Older children could whip cream and beat egg whites to make meringues. They could also learn how to use electric food processors with an adult.

Follow-up activities

∗   Mix and whisk paint.
∗   Put whisks in the dry sand to experiment with the patterns they make.
∗   Make pancakes with the children using a whisk to mix in the flour and the milk.

Links with home

Ask parents to let their children use a whisk and bubble bath when they have a bath at home.

Fastening up

Learning outcome

To use a range of small objects with increasing control.

Group size

Four children.

What you need

At least four different garments, with zip-fasteners, large buttons, poppers, laces, Velcro and so on.

Preparation

Spread the clothes out on a table so that their fastenings are uppermost. Undo the fastenings.

What to do

Talk about the clothes which the children are wearing. How do they fasten together? Ask each child if they can unfasten and fasten something on their own clothes. Then show the children the clothes you have placed on the table and ask them to have a go at fastening them up.

Encourage each child to have a go at each different type of fastening. If they find this easy, they could then try the clothes on and fasten them for each other and for themselves.

Put a chart on the wall so that the children can tick off all the different things they can do for themselves and for a friend.

Questions to ask

How does your jacket/cardigan/shirt/shoe fasten together? How do you get dressed in the morning? What clothes are your favourite ones? Why? How do you feel now you have fastened that up by yourself? What are you going to do next?

I can	Button a coat	Zip up a jacket	Tie a shoelace	Fasten a buckle	Tie a belt
Imran	✓	✓			✓
Zara	✓	✓	✓		✓
Georgia	✓	✓	✓	✓	✓
David	✓				✓
Neil	✓				✓
Severine	✓	✓			✓

For younger children

Younger children should start in a free-play situation with closed zips and Velcro before graduating to opening zips, buttons and finally laces. Very few children under four-years-old will be able to tie laces, as the dexterity involved is often beyond them.

For older children

Older children will be more able to tie laces in bows, thread laces through trainers and deal with hooks and eyes and other small and fiddly fastenings. Provide opportunities to try a full range of fastenings.

Follow-up activities

* Read the story *How do I put it on?* by Shigeo Watanabe (Red Fox).
* Provide a variety of fastenings for the doll's clothes in the role-play corner for free play.
* Make a collection of buttons and use them for sorting and matching activities.

Links with home

Send each child home with their list of successes so that parents can see what their child has achieved. Include an explanatory note with the sheet and ask parents to encourage their children to dress themselves at home.

Heads, arms and legs

Learning outcome

To develop cutting and sticking skills.

Group size

Six children

What you need

A small cardboard box for each child, Sellotape, scissors, glue stick, photocopiable page 90 (one copy for each child), a copy of the rhyme 'Heads, shoulders, knees and toes' on page 86.

Preparation

Collect suitable cardboard boxes (half-pound chocolate boxes of any shape are ideal).

What to do

Sing the rhyme 'Heads, shoulders, knees and toes'. Point out that each child has a head, a body, two legs and two arms, and that most people have the same shape. Give each child a copy of photocopiable page 90.

Suggest that the children use the small boxes as bodies and attach heads and arms and legs to them to make a figure. Encourage the children to cut out the pieces from the sheet of paper and stick the head and limbs to the box using Sellotape or glue.

Compliment the children on their achievements; do not tell a child that she has stuck anything in the wrong position if she is pleased with it. When the figures are finished, ask what each child would do differently next time, if anything at all.

Questions to ask

Where are you going to put that? What are you going to use? What shape is your box? What do you think was in it when it was full? What will it look like? How are you going to stick those arms and legs on?

For younger children

Young children may not have the dexterity skills needed to cut the paper pieces. An adult could lend a hand with the cutting and encourage the children to position and glue the pieces themselves.

For older children

Suggest that older children design some simple clothing for their figures. They could use pieces of material and fasten them to the limbs with staples, or they could punch holes in pieces of material and lace them together.

Follow-up activities

* Draw round one of the children and label the parts of the body on the drawing.
* Count arms, legs and heads of children, dolls and so on. What patterns can you find?
* Say the rhyme 'Hands and feet' on page 77.

Links with home

Parents could help their children count heads, legs and arms in their family. How many altogether?

chapter five

Co-ordination skills

Hand and eye co-ordination is vitally important for the development of writing, reading and drawing skills. In turn development of fine motor skills comes after development of the gross motor skills such as catching and throwing balls. Activities in this chapter reinforce the necessary skills

Wriggle through it!

Learning outcome

To move confidently through hoops.

Group size

Six children.

What you need

Three hoops, a large space for the children to move around freely. A copy of the song 'Wiggley Woo' on page 83.

Preparation

Sing the song 'Wiggley Woo' and practise wiggling.

What to do

Ask one child to stand and hold a hoop upright with its rim on the floor. Ask the other children to wriggle through this hoop in turn. Then ask two different children to hold hoops while all the others wriggle through the hoops. Lastly ask three children to hold hoops while the other three wriggle through each one. Give each child several turns to be both the 'hoop-holder' and the 'wriggler'.

Questions to ask

What did you like doing best? What happened when you held the hoop/when you were wriggling through it? What else can you do with a hoop?

For younger children

Younger children might find it easier to start this activity with you holding a hoop for them to wriggle through, they could then try the activity as above, but should take longer over each stage.

For older children

Older children could hold the hoops higher and have a different action to perform for each hoop, such as bunny-hopping through one, and doing a forward roll through another.

Follow-up activities

* Practise throwing beanbags into hoops laid on the floor. Then try throwing the beanbags through the hand-held hoop. Which is easiest?
* Practise jumping from one hoop to another laid flat on the floor, and very close together for young children.
* Practise bowling the hoops at a target.
* Use photocopiable page 91 to cut out a wriggly worm.

Links with home

Have a 'Well Done' board and display on it the names of all the children who tried hard to bowl the hoop or get the beanbags in the hoops. Encourage parents to look at the board.

Pat on the head

Learning outcome

To copy a pattern of movement.

Group size
Six children.

What you need
A carpeted area where the children can each have their own space to work.

Preparation
Check that the children in your group understand the words and can do the actions for patting and clapping.

What to do
Ask the children to kneel in a space of their own away from anyone else and ask them to copy what you do. Explain that if you clap, they should clap, and if you pat your head, they should do the same. Practice these two actions a few times, asking the children to keep their eyes on you so that they notice when you change from clapping to patting.

Introduce as many varieties of clapping and patting as you can devise. Pat the floor in front of you with both hands at the same time, then change to one hand at a time. Pat your shoulders, your chest, your tummy, your back (if you can!). Pat your knees, your thighs, and your elbows. Clap your hands in front of you, to each side, both high and low. Clap your hands in front of your body and behind. Ask the children what combinations of pats or claps they can think of.

Questions to ask
Tell me what different movements you could make with clapping and patting. What was easy? What was difficult? When did you notice the movement had changed? How did you feel when you forgot to change?

For younger children
Very young children should sing songs such as 'If you're happy and you know it' before trying to copy sequences of movement.

For older children
Older children could try to put together a repeating sequence of movements to make a simple routine, using the different sounds made by the different parts of their bodies to make a 'body orchestra'. They could perhaps perform their routine to the rest of the group.

Follow-up activities
∗   Learn some simple clapping and patting rhymes such as 'A sailor went to sea, sea, sea', and 'Hands and feet' on page 77.
∗   Put some simple percussion instruments on a table for the children to pat (tambourine or bongos).
∗   Clap the rhythm of each child's name at home time.

Links with home

Ask parents to teach their child any simple clapping games they remember from their own childhood.

Soft ball

Learning outcome

To use balls with increasing control.

Group size

Six children.

What you need

Soft foam balls, space for the children to move freely.

Preparation

Ensure you have enough balls for each child to have one.

What to do

Sit on the floor together and investigate what the balls are like. Encourage the children to squeeze them, twist them, squash them flat, throw them up, and bounce them on the floor.

Then ask the children to stand up and hold the balls under their chins, then hold them up in the air with a hand and then down on the ground with a foot. Encourage them to roll the balls with their hands gently and follow them. Say 'Don't let it get away, keep that ball right next to your hand. Now do the same with your foot. Keep the ball in contact, and push it gently around your space. Put your foot on top of it to stop it.'

Finally ask the children to find a partner and practise gently kicking the ball to each other, stopping it and returning it.

Questions to ask

What did you find easy? What did you find hard? What could you do with you hands? What could you do with your feet? Why does the ball keep moving? What's the best way to stop the ball? Why? What games can you play using a ball?

For younger children

Allow young children to have plenty of time playing freely with the sponge balls and finding out what they can do with them. You could then try the activity, leaving out the controlled kicking.

For older children

Older children could dribble the ball with both hands and feet around a series of cones or other obstacles. They could also practise throwing and kicking the ball into a bucket or a box.

Follow-up activities

* Put the soft balls into the water tray for the children to explore their properties as sponges.
* Print with sponge balls. What shape do you always get?
* Count the number of times a child can catch or bounce a ball.

Links with home

The children could make a target to take home to play with.

Hit it!

Learning outcome

To handle bats and balls with increasing control.

Group size

Eight to ten children.

What you need

Small round bats and soft balls.

Preparation

Take your group to a park or onto a grassy area for this activity.

What to do

Firstly give the children a bat and a ball each and let them play. After they have had some time to explore what they can do, call them all together and show them how to drop the ball onto the bat in order to hit it. Then see if they can hit a ball thrown to them.

Stand in the middle of a circle of children and throw the ball carefully to each in turn. Clap loudly if anyone succeeds in hitting it! Finally let the children choose which of the things they have tried they would like to practise, and let them have plenty of time to do this.

Questions to ask

What did you do with the bat and ball? What was the thing you liked best? Who did you play with? What did you play? What games do you play with a ball at home? How could you hit the target? What did you find easy? What was more difficult?

For younger children

Younger children need to have lots of opportunities to play with bats and balls, typically learning how to hold the bat against the floor and hitting a rolling ball before attempting to hit it in the air.

For older children

Older children can start to work in pairs, hitting the ball to each other, both in the air and bouncing off the ground. They can also try to hit a target drawn on an outside wall with coloured chalk

Follow-up activities

* Use plastic hockey sticks or small rounders bats to hit a ball along the ground.
* Show the children how to hit the ball by patting it with their hands.
* Suspend a ball or a beanbag on a string and let the children practise hitting it.

Links with home

Send a letter home asking if any parents can accompany you on your visit to the park with the children, to increase the adult to child ratio.

Where's the catch?

To develop hand-eye co-ordination.

Group size
Six children.

What you need
Soft plastic playballs (about 20cm in diameter), one between two children, space for throwing and catching a ball without obstruction.

Preparation
Preferably, take your group outdoors. If this is not possible, ensure that your chosen area does not have any projecting furniture which could hurt the children if they ran into it.

What to do
Sit in a circle with your group, and pass one ball from hand to hand around the circle, talking about its colour and its shape. Next ask the children to stand up, and you stand in the middle. Ask each child if they want to catch the ball, and throw it gently to each one in turn.

If any children cannot catch the ball, ask them to put their hands together and open in front of their chest. Gently throw the ball into the cradle they have made, and tell them to clasp the ball to their chest. Most children without a physical disability can catch at once using this method, and this greatly increases their confidence. They can then try to throw the ball for you to catch. This skill can then be practised with another child as their partner.

Questions to ask
What did you do with the ball? What happens if you don't catch it? What games can you play with a ball? Which is your favourite ball game? How many times could you catch the ball? What made it easy or hard to do? Why?

For younger children
Let younger children have plenty of time to experiment with throwing the ball and finding out how it moves and what they can do with it. Start the main activity when the children start to try to catch the ball.

For older children
Let older children practise catching. Encourage them to count the number of times they can catch the ball throwing it up in the air, against the wall and so on. Try using different sized balls.

Follow-up activities
∗ Try throwing and catching quoits or beanbags.
∗ Develop skills using a large football.
∗ Give plenty of time to practise catching an assortment of balls.

Links with home
Invite parents to come and watch the children throwing and catching balls. Ask them to practice throwing a ball gently for their child to catch at home.

Target practice

To develop hand-eye co-ordination by aiming at a target.

Group size
Six children.

What you need
Anything soft which can be thrown, such as balls of wool, beanbags, plastic balls.

Preparation
The children should have plenty of opportunities for free play with balls, before attempting this activity.

What to do
Draw a target on the wall outside, or pin a target to the wall indoors. This should measure about a metre across and could be a square, a circle or a triangle; even a flower or a dragon's face.

Ask the children to look at the target and throw their balls at it in turn. At first, praise the children for hitting the target anywhere, but then ask them to shout out which part of the target they are aiming for, such as the top, the bottom or the middle.

Questions to ask
What happened then? Why did you do that? Where did the ball go? Where did you want it to go? How can you stop the ball rolling away? What games can you play? Which one do you like best? Why? What would happen if the ball was square?

For younger children
Younger children could play freely with the balls, and you could join in their game. If appropriate, show them how to roll or kick the ball in any way they can.

For older children
Older children could work in pairs to use their rolling and kicking skills to deliver the ball to a suitable place for their partner to control.

Follow-up activities
∗ Roll and kick the ball at a target such as a cone in the middle of the floor.
∗ Use rolling with hands and kicking to weave through obstacles in a line.
∗ Try rolling a ball into a hoop on the floor. This needs good hand-eye co-ordination and steady force, but not too much.

Links with home

Ask children and their parents to look at home for pictures of people rolling and kicking balls. Display them all on a board with labels describing the action shown.

Filling up

Learning outcome

To handle appropriate tools and objects safely and with increasing control.

Group size

Eight children.

What you need

Dried pasta shapes, eight containers of increasing sizes from small to large (such as a stacking set of beakers), eight plastic spoons, a large unbreakable bowl.

Preparation

Put the dry pasta into the large bowl and place it within easy reach of the children.

What to do

Ask the children to use their spoons to transfer the pasta from the large bowl to fill the different sizes of container, choosing one each and filling it carefully. They should empty it in the same way and move on to another size of container to fill that.

Children find this activity very soothing and satisfying, and they learn a lot about capacity as well as developing their dexterity skills.

Questions to ask

What is pasta used for? What do we have to do to it before we can eat it? Have you tasted pasta? Do you like it? What are you going to do next? Why did that happen? Where does your mum or dad buy pasta from? What happens to pasta when we cook it? Why? Which container took longest to fill? Why?

For younger children

Use large pasta shapes such as cannelloni and encourage younger children just to use their hands to fill the containers first, then try using spoons.

For older children

Older children could half-fill as well as fill their containers, perhaps counting how many pasta shapes they can fit in. Encourage them to estimate how many pieces of pasta would fill each container.

Follow-up activities

* Use different materials such as woolly pom-poms, strings of paper-clips or Unifix cubes to fill pots.
* Put containers, spoons, ladles and scoops in the water-tray so that children can spoon water to fill the containers.
* Cook the pasta and let it cool. Do the activity again with the cooked pasta. What is different?
* Use photocopiable page 92 to order bells for size, either by cutting and sticking or by writing numbers.

Links with home

Ask the children to bring in empty containers from home to use in this activity.

Twisting away

To handle appropriate construction toys with increasing control.

Group size

Eight to ten children.

What you need

A construction set which has lots of nuts and bolts, tools to use with them, such as Bauplay, Brio-Mec or LEGO Toolo. A comfortable place for the children to sit and play.

Preparation

Make sure that you have enough pieces and tools in your set for each child. Separate the nuts and bolts from the larger pieces.

What to do

Sit with your group and ask them how you could join two pieces of the construction toy together using the screwdrivers to fasten and unfasten the nuts and bolts.

Ask the children to show you how they would do it, and see who can use the screwdriver rather than just their fingers. Talk about how the pieces fit together. Look carefully together at the way the screwdriver fits into the head of the bolt.

Give the children plenty of time to experiment with the pieces and discover what they can do with the tools.

Questions to ask

What is a screwdriver used for in your house? What are you going to do with that piece? How did you do that? What other tools could we use? Where should we keep the tools to make sure they are safe?

For younger children

Give younger children a few large diameter nuts and bolts to fasten together with their fingers before attempting to use tools.

For older children

Older children could use small versions of real tools for sawing and drilling wood (such as Balsa) and hammering nails as well as screwing screws into it. For safety reasons this activity must be closely supervised by an adult.

Links with home

Ask a parent skilled in DIY to drill some thick pieces of wood with different sizes of holes for the children to practise fitting the right sized screw to each hole.

Follow-up activities

* Print using nuts and bolts, rolling them across the paper as well as using the heads.

* Use nuts and bolts with clay or dough. Is it easy to push them in? Does it hold together?

* Make a collection of objects held together with screws and let the children take them to pieces and talk about what is inside.

How high can you go?

Learning outcome

To develop hand-eye co-ordination by building a tower with bricks.

Group size

Four children.

What you need

A set of plain solid bricks of the same shape (cubes or cuboids), a comfortable carpeted area.

Preparation

Ask the children to find the bricks and get them out from where they are stored.

What to do

Build a tower by placing the single bricks exactly on top of each other. Build the highest one you can, until it falls down.

Encourage the children to build the highest tower they can. Tell them to take their time and put their bricks carefully one on top of the other, to see how tall they can make their tower.

Then encourage the children to see what happens if they lift the bricks and place them as quickly as they can. Which tower is most stable? Discuss what you have discovered with the children.

Questions to ask

Which way of building worked best? Why? What else could you do to help your tower stay standing? Who made the tallest tower? What was it as tall as? What would happen if you blew on your tower? What would happen if you built it on a slope?

For younger children.

It will be a triumph for younger children if they can succeed in placing three bricks in a tower without knocking them over! Encourage all the children to achieve this.

For older children

Older children enjoy using many sizes and shapes of bricks to make tall constructions. They could be set problems such as using a timer to see who could build the tower with a certain number of bricks in the shortest time.

Follow-up activities

* Make a picture of a tower. Ask the children to cut squares of gummed paper and stick them one above the other to make a high tower.
* Count the bricks in a tower. Put sticky labels on each one to show the number of bricks, starting with 1 at the bottom. Take some away. How many are left?
* Stack (plastic) coins in piles in the role-play shop. Stack tins and packets on top of each other as though in the supermarket.

Links with home

Recommend some games which develop hand-eye co-ordination, such as Jackstraws, Ludo or Snakes and Ladders; provide these for parents to borrow .

Threading it through

Learning outcome

To thread beads in a pattern of colours.

Group size

Eight children.

What you need

Round wooden beads of different colours, threading laces with covered ends in assorted colours, gummed paper in the same colours, plastic saucers or dishes, cards (20cm × 5cm), scissors, large button, black biro.

Preparation

Draw around the button several times on a piece of gummed paper. Stack all the colours of paper underneath each other and cut out one shape to provide circles of all the available colours. Use these coloured circles to make simple repeating patterns along a line; make up cards each with a different pattern. Together with the children, sort the beads into sets of different colours.

What to do

Ask the children to each make a necklace using the coloured beads. Show them how to thread through the beads, but then encourage them to work independently. You may need to tie a knot at the end of the lace so that the children can keep the beads on the thread.

Once the children have made one necklace, ask them to choose one of the cards which you have made up and match the beads to the pattern, continuing it to the end of the lace.

Questions to ask

What colours are in your necklace? How do you put the beads on? What pattern is that? What happens when the beads fall on the floor? Do you like to wear a necklace?

For younger children

Younger children should be encouraged to explore what they can do with the beads and laces, and be given plenty of time to play freely.

For older children

Older children can work with smaller beads and blunt needles, even making friendship bracelets with plaited strands of small beads.

Follow-up activities

∗ Make your own threading cards by gluing some attractive pictures to card, laminating them and punching holes in them. Encourage the children to thread laces through the holes to make patterns.
∗ Thread hollow pasta onto soft string to make necklaces.
∗ Thread a skipping rope (without handles) through some large items like plastic bricks or quoits.

Links with home

As parents come into nursery, inform them about one activity you will be doing today, and suggest they ask their child about it at home.

chapter six

Balance and awareness of space

Children who lack spatial awareness can have problems with reading and writing as a result. Balance is all about controlling the body either while still or moving and is an important element for young children to attain. Both areas are essential elements in a child's development.

Frog hopping

Learning outcome

To balance on a bench and jump onto a mat.

Group size
Ten children.

What you need
A low bench, the song 'Five little speckled frogs' (can be spoken) on page 87, a small mat.

Preparation
Put the mat in front of the low bench to act as a pool.

What to do
Sing or say the rhyme with the children. When they are familiar with the words, ask for five volunteers to stand on the bench to take it in turns to jump into the pool as the other five sing the song. Then the other five children take a turn to be frogs.

Encourage the children to take their turn, but do not insist if there is a child who does not want to have a turn yet.

Questions to ask
What did you like best about the song? What did you do first? What did you like doing? What do real frogs look like? What do baby frogs look like? Where do you find them? What other songs can you sing?

For younger children
Younger children may find it easier to try the activity standing on the floor and concentrate on jumping into the pool.

For older children
Older children still enjoy this song, and could be expected to balance in a squat and jump high with a controlled two-footed landing into the pool.

Follow-up activities
∗ Do a similar activity with a different rhyme and a different movement such as 'I saw a slippery, slithery snake' on page 78.
∗ Use photocopiable page 93 and cut out and stick the frogs on the log.
∗ Read *The Wide-mouthed Frog* by Keith Faulkner (Madcap Books).
∗ Visit a pond in spring with the children and collect some frogs carefully in collecting pots. Look at them closely and be sure to put them back where they came from safely.

Links with home

Photocopy the words of 'Five little speckled frogs' and send them home for parents to have fun with their children.

Rock and roll

To move confidently and imaginatively with increasing skill.

Group size
Six children.

What you need
Sufficient space to move around freely, a mat for each child to lie on.

Preparation
Ensure the children are dressed comfortably and that they remove shoes and socks. Always do a warm-up exercise with the children before starting any physical activity. Try some gentle stretching and jogging.

What to do
Put out the mats and ask the children to each sit on their own mat. Show them how to bring their knees up to

their chests and clasp them with their arms. Ask the children to bend their heads over to make a curled shape.

Next, ask the children if they can rock backwards and roll onto their backs, keeping their arms around their legs. Can they rock forwards and backwards? Can they rock from side to side? Now ask them to kneel on their mats and curl up into balls. Can they roll from side to side now?

After they have done this, ask the children if they can stretch out and roll over. Give them time to explore this, as they will have great fun. Ask them to roll towards a target, such as the door or a picture on the wall.

Questions to ask
What did you like doing best? Why? What did you think was funny? What was hard to do? How does it feel when you are rolling over? Have you ever rolled down a hill? Where else would it be fun to roll? How would you feel if you rolled for a long time?

For younger children
Younger children may find it difficult to roll forwards and backwards, and should concentrate on rolling from side to side.

For older children
Older children can create a sequence of rolls forwards and backwards as well as side to side. They could also practise synchronised rolling where they all face inwards in a circle and one person shouts 'left' or 'right' and everyone rolls that way.

Links with home
Ask the children to show their parents what they can do.

Follow-up activities
* Sing 'Ten in the bed' while rolling on the floor.
* Use a parachute and take turns to roll under it while the rest of the group lift it up.
* Read the stories *Ten in the bed* and *Ten out of bed* by Penny Dale (Walker Books).

Growing seeds

To move imaginatively to music.

Group size
Six children.

What you need
A cassette recorder and a cassette of the first part of Greig's 'Morning' from *Peer Gynt*, sufficient space for the children to move.

Preparation
Plant some quick-growing seeds (such as peas) indoors and let the children watch them start to grow. Dig one or two up so that the children can look closely at the roots and the green shoot itself.

Ensure the children are dressed comfortably and that they remove shoes and socks.

What to do
Play the music and ask the children what it makes them think of. Remind them of the seeds they have seen and ask them to pretend to be a seed, rolled up very small, growing roots first (feet) then growing up into a shoot (arms), followed by buds (hands), a flower (stand up, open arms and smile!) and then a seed pod (whole body) and more seeds.

You might find it useful to use a script, such as:

First the tiny seed lies in the soil.
It starts to grow roots so that it can feed itself.
Then a shoot starts to grow upwards and upwards to the light.
The stem starts to put out leaves.
Then a bud.
The bud bursts open to show a beautiful flower.
The flower dies and the seed pod swells up until
Pop! it bursts and lots more seeds lie on the ground waiting to grow...

Questions to ask
What flowers do you have in your garden? What else grows in your garden? What do you need when you plant seeds? What helps seeds to grow?

What grows from a seed first? Why? Who eats seeds? What seeds do you eat? What type of seed do you think tastes best?

For younger children
Play the music and ask very young children to listen and then move around the way they think the music is telling them.

For older children
Older children may be able to devise a script for themselves, and could take turns to read it aloud while the rest of the group performs.

Follow-up activities
* Read *The Tiny Seed* by Eric Carle (Picture Puffin).
* Make a seed collage, sticking down nut husks and dried pulses to make patterns.
* Collect examples of different moods of music, such as Wagner's 'Ride of the Walkyrie' or Boccherini's 'Minuet' and let the children create a dance about the weather.

Links with home

Put your topic web for the term up on display and illustrate it with photographs as the children do the activities.

Streamers

Learning outcome

To move confidently and imaginatively using small equipment with increasing control.

Group size

Six children.

What you need

Old net curtains, pieces of dowel (about 25cm in length) one for each child and one for you, glue, scissors, a cassette recorder and some gentle music such as *Cavatina* (John Williams) and some exciting music such as Ravel's *Bolero*.

Preparation

Cut the net into strips (about 10cm wide, the full length of the curtain). Encourage the children to help you glue the strips of net firmly to the ends of the dowel pieces, wrapping each one around the stick two or three times to make streamers.

What to do

Give the streamers to the children and let them explore their properties; waving them around, running with them and so on. Suggest they all run in the same direction to prevent collisions!

Next, gather your group together and demonstrate some high movements, some low movements and some movements around the middle of the body. Make movements forwards and backwards, from side to side and up and down.

Then ask the children to listen to the music and to move their streamers in the way they think the music is 'telling' them.

Questions to ask

What are you going to do with your streamer? Tell me what movements you could make. What does your streamer look like when you are running? What happens to it when you are still? What does the music make you think of? Why?

For younger children

Let young children play freely with the streamers, perhaps out-of-doors, running around and finding what shapes they can make with them first.

You could then try the main activity when you think they are ready for it.

For older children

Older children could try to put together a repeating sequence of movements to make a simple dance.

Follow-up activities

* Watch a video of rhythmic gymnastics using ribbons, then see if the children can copy some of the movements made.
* Go outside and fly your streamers on a windy day; can the children copy the movements made by the streamers in the wind?
* Encourage the children to draw patterns of streamers on paper; encourage large arm movements and swirling patterns.

Links with home

Invite parents in to watch a 'performance' by your group.

Upside-down!

Learning outcome

To explore the concept of being upside-down.

Group size
Eight children.

What you need

An open space where the children can move around safely.

Preparation

Ensure the children are comfortably dressed and have bare feet. Make sure the children always warm-up before exercise. If there is not much space indoors, take them outside for a walk, jog and gentle stretch before you start.

What to do

Ask the children to spread out in the space available and to stretch up as tall as they can. Talk about how we stand upright with our heads at the top and our feet on the floor. Ask the children if they would like to see the world in a different way; upside-down.

Encourage them to bend their knees and bend over to look between their legs at the upside-down world. Ask them to describe what they can see. Now ask them to make a bridge shape. They can see an upside-down view of the room between their legs. Ask the children to try and move around the room in their bridge shapes. What does it feel like to see things upside-down? Is it hard to move?

Cool down by asking the children to lie on their backs and look up at the ceiling, explain that this is also another view of the room.

Questions to ask.

What were we doing this morning? What did the world look like when you were upside-down? What did you like doing best? Why? What could you do if you had to be upside-down all the time? How would you eat and drink?

For younger children

Younger children could just try bending over to look at the world upside-down.

For older children

Older children can develop this activity into forward rolls. With close adult supervision they can also hang upside-down on wall bars and suitable gymnastic equipment.

Follow-up activities

* Use the photocopiable matching sheet Topsy turvy on page 94 and match the upside-down items to the ones which are the right way up!
* Bake some upside-down cakes with the children.
* Ask the children to draw upside-down pictures.

Links with home

Put an upside-down display on the notice board where parents will be sure to see it.

Musical statues with a difference

Learning outcome

To hold a balance for a short time.

Group size

Eight to ten children.

What you need

A cassette player and a cassette of continuous music for the children to dance and move about to.

Preparation

Ensure the children are suitably dressed for physical activity and have bare feet.

What to do

Ask the children to space themselves out around the room. Explain that when the music is playing they should dance around the room and when the music stops they should freeze like a statue. Tell them that you will then pick out one child who is holding very still in a balancing position (on their toes, on one leg, on one arm and one leg and so on).

Try the activity and when you pick out a child ask all the others to gather around and look at the selected child and clap. Then start the music and do it again until everyone has had a turn at being the statue.

Questions to ask

Why was that game fun? What did you do? What did your friend do? Which balance do you think is easiest? Which is the hardest to do? What did you think of the music? What did it make you want to do?

For younger children

Younger children will find it very difficult to stay still for more than a few seconds, and balance will be difficult. Just ask the children to stop when the music stops and stand still; this will be a feat of balance in itself for young children.

For older children

Older children will have developed their balancing skills and will be able to hold more complex balances.

Follow-up activities

* Practise balancing on a low plank or bench placed near the role-play area.
* Provide ballet clothes (for both sexes) and books such as *Lili at Ballet* by Rachel Isadora (Mammoth) which show balancing in dance.
* Provide a full-length unbreakable mirror so that children can practice freezing in a posture.

Links with home

Ask parents if they have any discarded ballet clothes which they could give to you. One of the parents may even be a dancer who could come and show the children the balancing positions used in dance.

On your head!

Learning outcome

Developing control in balancing a beanbag.

Group size

Eight children.

What you need

A beanbag for each child, an open space (outdoors or indoors), equipment such as a hoop, a cone and a skipping rope.

Preparation

Place your equipment to make an obstacle course for the children to negotiate, going into and out of the hoop, round the cone and stepping over the skipping rope laid flat on the ground.

What to do

Hand out the beanbags to the children and ask them what they can do with them. Encourage them to think of as many ways as they can to hold them and throw them.

Next show the children how to balance a beanbag on your head and walk without letting it fall off. Encourage them to try to balance their beanbags and to walk about without touching them with their hands.

When they have had plenty of time to try walking and balancing the beanbags, suggest that they try the obstacle course, demonstrating first the movements you want them to make around the chosen obstacles, without letting the beanbags fall off.

Questions to ask

What can you do with your beanbag? Why is it hard to do? What are you going to do next? How did you feel when it fell off? What did you do to make that happen? How can you make it stay on your head?

For younger children

If younger children can balance a beanbag on their heads for even a short while, they are doing very well. Introduce the cone only to start with, and encourage the children to walk carefully around it if they want to. Allow those who do not wish to do this to continue with free-play.

For older children

Older children should be able to cope with more obstacles and more difficult ones such as a raised rope or a step up and down.

Follow-up activities

* Ask the children to balance other items on their heads such as quoits, plastic bricks, or small hoops.
* Balance a beanbag on their shoulders, backs, a bent arm or a foot.
* Encourage the children to try to run while balancing a foam ball on a cupped palm.

Links with home

Organise a potato-and-spoon race at sports day and ask parents to join in.

Tightrope walkers!

Learning outcome

To develop balance using skipping ropes.

Group size
Four children.

What you need
Skipping ropes (without wooden handles), an open space such as a carpeted area, a book or video showing tightrope walkers.

Preparation
Try to find a book or video with pictures of a tightrope walker.

What to do
Talk about the book or the video you have seen and discuss the things which tightrope walkers can do with their arms to help them balance. Ask the children if they would like to be tightrope walkers themselves.

Lay the skipping rope on the floor in a fairly straight line and ask for a volunteer to walk across it. Explain to the children that if they fall off, they have to sit on the floor and wait for another turn. Encourage each child to take a turn while the others watch. Clap loudly when someone makes it all the way across the tightrope to the other side.

Questions to ask
What does a tightrope walker do? Why is it hard to do? How would you feel if you were a tightrope walker? What would you do if you started to wobble? How could you learn to be a tightrope walker? Where would you go to learn?

For younger children
Draw a chalk line on the floor outside for younger children to walk along instead.

For older children
Older children could try making loops and waves with longer skipping ropes, and following the pattern to the end. They can also follow a line of loops and other patterns drawn in chalk.

Follow-up activities
∗ Balance along a low bench and jump off the end.
∗ Paint a spiral on the ground of your outdoor play area and put a star or a flower in the centre.

Links with home

Suggest that parents try some balancing games with their children at home. They may like to hold their child's hand as they walk carefully along a low garden wall, or encourage them to balance on one leg when they are getting dried after swimming or a bath!

In a circle

To develop an awareness of space and other people.

Group size

Eight to ten children.

What you need

Space for the children to hold hands in a circle, the words of a ring game such as 'There was a princess long ago' or 'Ring-o-Ring-o-Roses' (both in *This Little Puffin* compiled by Elizabeth Matterson (Penguin)).

Preparation

Practise the words of the song with the children so that they know it before they act it out.

What to do

Encourage the children to form a circle, asking them to stretch their arms out and make the largest circle they can and still hold hands. Talk about the shape they have made, pointing out who is next to whom, then ask the children to release hands and keep the circle shape.

Sing the song and do the actions, reminding the children that they should come back to the circle shape when they have finished. Try to make a bigger circle by moving backwards as a group but not holding hands. Try to make a smaller circle by moving forwards and closer together.

Do this a few times, and then finish by trying 'The hokey cokey'.

Questions to ask

Who was standing next to you? Who was on your other side? What did you like doing best? Why? How did we make a circle? What part would you like to play? How did we make the circle bigger? How did we make it smaller?

For younger children

Just joining hands together to make a circle and playing a ring game is quite enough for younger children. You may find that they only want to hold hands with the person on one side, and actually getting a circle formed will be difficult enough!

For older children

All children love to play ring games, but older children can play games requiring more physical ability, such as 'I sent a letter to my love'.

Follow-up activities

∗ Form a conga line as another way of developing awareness of space and other people.
∗ Walk around the room as a group, all shaking hands with any person walking towards you.
∗ Run, jump, skip or hop about the room, but if you touch someone else, you must sit down and cross your legs.

Links with home

Ask for volunteers to come and play ring games with the children.

Moving feet

Learning outcome

To explore balance and movement using feet.

Group size

Eight to ten children.

What you need

An open space in which to move.

Preparation

Ask the children to take their shoes and socks off by themselves if they can.

What to do

Tell the children that they must listen carefully and that you will tell them what to do. First ask them to sit down on the floor, then stand up, then sit down and so on.

Then ask the children if they can walk on the spot for a while, then jog, then hop, then jump. Once they have done each of these things, vary them. Tell the children to try to walk backwards, to walk with their legs wide apart, or as if with their knees tied together. Ask them to walk with one foot in front of the other, or sideways.

Ask if the children can jog slowly, lifting their knees high in the air, or stand on one leg and lift their other leg to the front, side and back. Can they jump with feet together and then apart, lifting their arms up and down as they do?

Questions to ask

How do you feel when you have been doing all this exercise? What did you like doing best? Why? What was easy? What was hard? What did you do with your feet? What else can you do? What other parts of your body were you using?

For younger children

Do not attempt to try all these ideas in one session with younger children but spend some time on the basics first; learning how to walk on the spot, learning how to hop and so on, possibly to music.

For older children

Older children could start to take their weight on their hands in bunny-hops or sideways jumps which will develop into cartwheels.

Follow-up activities

* Talk about the heart which pumps blood around our bodies. Ask the children to feel their heart beating faster after exercise.
* See how many hops or jumps each child can do while the sand runs through an egg-timer.
* Set up your role-play area as an exercise studio.

Links with home

Ask the children to demonstrate to their parents what they have done when they get home.

chapter seven

Using malleable materials

Children learn through their senses, and by working their will on objects. There is nothing more satisfying than the touch of wet sand or smooth dough especially with an added smell or texture. Activities using clay, dough, sand, and mud are all included in this chapter to develop skills.

Slime!

Learning outcome

To experiment with an unusual texture.

Group size

Eight to ten children.

What you need

The recipe and ingredients for slime, food colouring (pink appears interesting and green looks disgusting and is very attractive to some small children), a water-tray or bowl to hold the slime, aprons and protective covering for surfaces, spoons, sticks, scoops, pouring vessels.

Preparation

With the children's help mix the slime together and place it in the water tray or bowl.

Recipe for slime

3 cups of Lux soap flakes
Approx 1 litre of warm water
Food colouring
To make – Sprinkle the flakes into the water and whisk until slimey froth is formed.

What to do

Put on protective aprons and allow the children to group around the tray holding the slime.

While they are playing in the slime, ask them to show you what it does and what it feels like when they touch it. Encourage them to lift the slime and let it drop, to scoop up the slime and let it slither down, and to put slime into the jugs and pour it from one into the other.

Show them what happens when you poke the slime with a stick and then lift and twist it around. Do the same with a spoon.

Questions to ask

What does the slime look like? How does it feel? What does it smell like? What happens if you lift some up? How would you feel if you took a bath in slime? What can you do with the slime? What does it make you think of?

For younger children

As always, younger children need plenty of time for free play first, so that they can fully explore the properties of the texture of the slime.

For older children

Slime is also attractive to older children, who tend to be more able to manipulate it. They could smear the slime onto paper and then draw a slime-beast on it when dry.

Follow-up activities

∗ Read *Slimy Book* by Babette Cole (Cape).
∗ Go for a slug and snail hunt and look carefully at them.
∗ Read 'My day out', a poem about touch, on page 77.

Links with home

Take photographs of the children playing with the slime and pin them on a notice board for parents to see.

Mud pies

Learning outcome

To handle malleable materials with confidence.

Group size

Four children.

What you need

A bag of peat-free compost, a water tray or large plastic bath, wooden mixing spoons, water, rakes, buckets and spades, aprons.

Preparation

Put a small amount of water in the water tray or bath and put the dry peat-free compost into it. At first it will float on the top and remain dry. Ensure that all the children put on an apron.

What to do

Using the wooden mixing spoons and bare hands, ask the children to join you in mixing the compost with the water. When the compost has been thoroughly soaked and resembles thick mud, encourage the children to mould it with their hands and make it into piles. Talk about the texture of the mud, and its colour.

Introduce the rakes and spades from the sand and ask the children if they can make patterns in the mud. Introduce buckets and ask the children if they can make mud pies instead of sand pies.

Finish by making sure the children all wash their hands thoroughly.

Questions to ask

What are your hands like when you've been playing in the mud? What does the mud feel like? What would happen if you spilled the mud? What could you do? What patterns can you make in the mud? What do you like doing best in the mud?

For younger children

Give younger children plenty of time to experiment with and experience the feel of the mud with their bare hands. They could then go on to use buckets and spades and other sand toys for free play.

For older children

Ask older children to write about how the mud felt to them, and perhaps even work in a group to write a poem about mud.

Follow-up activities

∗ Mix wood-shavings and sawdust together with water to make a swamp. Let the children use model dinosaurs to encourage imaginative play.

∗ Go outside and dig in the soil. Look carefully at the things you find.

∗ Make a wormery in a large plastic jar with layers of sand, soil, leaves and well-rotted manure. Put some worms inside and position it in a cool place, covering the outside with dark paper or fabric. Look at what happens to the layers.

Links with home

Photocopy the story 'The mud hole' on page 81 and suggest that parents read it as a bedtime story.

Dry patterns

Learning outcome

To draw patterns and pictures using dry materials.

Group size
Six children.

What you need
Six shallow trays (use different primary colours to add another dimension to the activity), dry sand or salt (enough for a thin layer over the base of each tray), some blank card (about A5 size), a thick black felt-tipped pen.

Preparation
Draw some patterns on the cards for the children to copy (see below).

What to do
Ask the children if they can use their fingers to draw a picture in the sand or salt. Demonstrate how they can draw on the trays and then just shake them slightly to clear the surface when they have filled up all the space. Give them plenty of time to experiment with this.

Then ask if they could copy a pattern, and let each child choose one of the cards to follow, and then swap it for another when they have finished. Again, the children should be given plenty of time to play with the patterns in the sand and salt.

Questions to ask
What have you drawn there? Which pattern did you find easy? Which one was hard? Why? How does it feel when you are drawing? How do you make it clear again? What colour is your drawing? Why?

For younger children
Allow younger children plenty of opportunity to make marks freely in the trays.

For older children
Older children can practise writing their names and making correct letter-shapes on the trays, as well as drawing pictures and patterns.

Follow-up activities
* Try some finger-painting.
* Trace over patterns on tracing paper using felt-tipped pens.
* Use flattened damp clay and gouge patterns with fingers.

Links with home

Invite parents to stay and watch the way the children work with the dry materials. Consider holding a workshop on early writing skills.

The queen of hearts

Learning outcome

To assemble and bake jam tarts.

Group size

Six children.

What you need

To make approximately 12 tarts: 200g margarine, 400g flour, water or milk to mix, jam, teaspoon, rolling-pins and pastry-cutters, baking tray, oven, plain and gold card, red metallic foil, scissors, aprons.

Preparation

Make card templates of a heart in different sizes. Make an example of a crown using a strip of gold card decorated with red foil heart-shapes. Cut strips of card for children to use.

What to do

Provide the materials for the children to make crowns. Show them how to cut around the template, but encourage them to do the cutting and sticking themselves, even if the resulting heart shapes are almost unrecognisable.

When the crowns are complete, say the rhyme 'The queen of hearts' together, wearing the crowns and doing the actions.

Ask the children to put on aprons and with them still wearing the crowns, make the jam tarts together. Start by measuring out the ingredients and mixing the pastry together with the children. Let them take turns to stir the ingredients. Encourage the children to roll out the pastry themselves, use the cutters to make the jam tart cases, and fill them with jam themselves.

Bake the tarts for 20 minutes at 180°C (350°F, Gas Mark 4) and leave plenty of time for the jam to cool down before the children eat them.

Questions to ask

How are you going to make your crown? What will you do first? What are you going to use to stick it? How did you make your pastry? What did you use? What happened to the knave of hearts in the rhyme?

For younger children

Younger children may find it very difficult to cut a heart-shape, so you should consider cutting these out in advance for them to use.

For older children

Encourage older children to write down the ingredients they used, and ask them to try writing out the nursery rhyme from memory.

Follow-up activities

* Use photocopiable page 95 to invite children to write the first line of the nursery rhyme using a 'look, cover, write, check' approach.
* Leave the crowns in the role-play corner, and add robes and baking trays to encourage drama based on the rhyme.
* Ask the children what other nursery rhymes they know; maybe have a concert.

Links with home

Send a copy of the rhyme 'The queen of hearts' home for parents to enjoy together with their children.

Plasticine pictures

Learning outcome

To use Plasticine to produce a three-dimensional picture.

Group size

Six children.

What you need

Plasticine (in a variety of colours), A4 card, tools for working with the Plasticine, paintbrushes (size 8), PVA glue, magnifying glasses.

Preparation

This activity is particularly suitable in the autumn as you need to collect seasonal foliage and berries. Make sure you do not collect any poisonous varieties. Sort the berries into different types.

What to do

Ask the children to look at the berries using the magnifying glasses. Talk about what you can see, the size and colour of the berries, the different shapes of the leaves and so on. Ensure that the children do not put the berries in their mouths.

Ask the children if they can make a picture of the berries using the Plasticine. Show the children the tools and how to use them to model the berries, then show them how to glue the Plasticine to the card so that it creates a three-dimensional effect.

When the children have finished their pictures, ask them to paint more PVA glue over the top to give their sculpture a shiny finish.

Questions to ask

What shapes were the berries you made? How did you make them? What did you do first? How did you soften the Plasticine? What did you use to make that pattern? Are you pleased with your picture? What are you going to do with it?

For younger children

With younger children focus on looking carefully at the berries and then working with green and red Plasticine on a board.

For older children

Encourage older children to make very detailed pictures in Plasticine and then mount them into frames.

Follow-up activities

* Make sketches of brightly-coloured berries on black paper using pastels or chalks.
* Make gingerbread men or other biscuits which can be decorated using tools.
* Make plaster casts of model figures or plaques for the children to paint.

Links with home

Give parents the recipe for salt dough from page 61 and ask them to make some and use it at home with their child, perhaps over a long holiday.

Clay pots

Learning outcome

To explore clay as a malleable material.

Group size

Six children.

What you need

Terracotta clay or Newclay (available from artists' suppliers), sticks and tools (for scratching patterns in the clay), aprons, Formica boards for each child.

Preparation

Ensure that your clay is suitable for the children to work with. If it is dry, soak it in water and wrap it in a damp cloth overnight. Make a thumb-pot in advance to show the children.

What to do

Give the children plenty of time to explore the properties of the clay. Let them pummel it, roll it and poke it with sticks. This exploration could take place over several weeks if the clay is only available for part of the week.

When the children are ready, show them the pot you have made. Show them how to take a ball of clay about the size of their fist, and how to push their thumbs into the middle and smooth out a hollow, squeezing up the sides.

Finally, show them how to decorate their pots by scratching patterns onto the outside. Mark the base of each pot with the child's initials. Leave the pots to dry.

Questions to ask

How does the wet clay feel? What can you make with it? What did you like doing best? What sort of patterns could you make? What did you use to make the patterns? What are you going to do with your finished pot?

For younger children

Younger children appreciate the tactile qualities of the clay and should be encouraged to manipulate it in whatever way they wish, without being expected to produce an object.

For older children

If you have access to a kiln, older children would probably enjoy having their pots fired to the biscuit stage.

Follow-up activities

* Mix clay with water to form a thick, viscous liquid. Put it in the water tray to provide an alternative pouring material.

* Roll out tiles of clay and encourage the children to press patterns on them using small bricks or cubes.

* Make balls of clay into ladybirds or hedgehogs by pinching them to a shape and then scratching with modelling tools.

* Read the poem 'Clay days' on page 79 to the children.

Links with home

Put up a list of all the different things the children can do with clay, and display it on a notice board to draw the parents' attention to the different skills their children are developing using clay.

Shaving foam

Learning outcome

To discover the properties of shaving foam as a malleable material.

Group size

Eight to ten children.

What you need

A can of spray shaving foam, trays or smooth boards (which will not spoil when wet), some alphabet letters (wood or plastic ones are ideal, but laminated paper ones are acceptable).

Preparation

Cover the surface of each tray with shaving foam. Check that none of the children have allergies to soap products.

What to do

Place the alphabet letters close to the trays of foam and encourage the children to choose a letter and trace it in the foam.

Show the children the correct way to form the letters, starting in the correct places. The foam can easily be smoothed over if the child makes a mistake. Children often enjoy the tactile effect and pleasant smell of the foam bubbles which encourages a high level of concentration, even in children who do not normally want to sit and write.

Questions to ask

What does the foam feel like? What can you do with it? What are you going to write now? Which is the easiest letter to write? Which is the hardest? Why? What is the foam usually used for? Who uses it? When?

For younger children

Encourage younger children to make shapes of any kind in the foam. Only introduce them to the idea of letter shapes when they have had plenty of free play.

For older children

Older children can write words and draw elaborate pictures in the foam.

Follow-up activities

✱ Encourage the children to try to form letters with foam.
✱ Colour the foam and let the children use it to make prints on paper.

Links with home

Prepare sheets which show the correct way to form letters (one large letter per sheet). Suggest that parents might like to take a different letter home each week to practise with their child writing over the letter using lots of colours.

Textured dough

Learning outcome

To explore texture through the use of malleable materials.

Group size

Eight children.

What you need

The recipe and ingredients for play dough, poppy seeds, dry rice or lentils, food colouring (optional), cutters, rolling pins, knives (blunt) and so on.

Preparation

Mix the dough according to the recipe, and add the seeds with the dry ingredients. Add food colouring if desired.

What to do

Ask the children to roll the dough between their hands and ask them to describe how it feels. Young children often do not have the vocabulary for describing touch, and you may need to suggest words to them, for example dry/ wet.

Recipe for play dough

200g plain flour
1 tbsp vegetable oil
100g salt
300 mls water
2 tsps cream of tartar
Food colouring
To make – Put all the ingredients into a pan on a very low heat until a soft texture is achieved, stirring continuously. When cool, keep in an airtight tin and it will keep for about three months.

Then encourage them to roll the dough out into a sausage with their hands, talking about how the dough looks and feels while they are doing it. The dough can then be rolled flat with rolling pins and cut with cutters. Explore its lumpy texture further by putting it on the back of their hands, their cheeks and so on. Remind the children that they must not eat the dough.

Questions to ask

What is different about this dough? What has it got in it? How does it feel? What can you do with it? What sort of dough do you like best? Why? Who makes pastry in your house? Do you help?

For younger children

Younger children find it difficult to talk about sensory experiences. If this is the case, allow them to enjoy exploring the dough without being questioned.

For older children

Older children might like to experiment with adding other seeds and grains to make dough. They could also make bread with currants in it.

Follow-up activities

* Use a 'feely' box or bag to encourage children to talk about what they can feel but not see.
* Make a 'feely' table by placing pieces of material such as fur, velvet and satin, together with sandpaper and other unusual textures together.
* Paint pictures using glue and sprinkling seeds, sand, sugar or grains to make a 'feely' picture.
* Say the poem 'Making bread' on page 79 to the children.

Links with home

Ask the children to bring objects from home for the 'feely' table.

Scented dough

Learning outcome

To explore the malleable qualities of scented dough.

Group size

Eight to ten children.

What you need

The recipe and ingredients for salt dough, a selection of scents (curry powder, fruit essence, ground herbs, essential flower oils and so on), plastic knives, forks, pastry-cutters, rolling pins and moulds.

Preparation

Decide which scent you will use. Use different scents, varying the approach with textured dough (see page 60) and coloured dough (add food colouring to salt dough).

What to do

Make the dough with the children. You could ask them to choose which of three pre-selected scents they want to put in their dough this week. Encourage the children to talk about the scent of the dough and how it makes them feel, and let them play freely with the dough, making whatever models they want to.

Ask the children to smell their hands after playing with the dough. Reinforce throughout that although the dough smells nice they must not put any in their mouths to taste it.

Questions to ask

What does this smell make you think of? How does it make you feel? What smells do you like? What smells do you think are nasty? Why? What did you make with the dough? Who did you make it for? What are you going to do with it?

For younger children

Younger children may not need extra help and will enjoy playing freely with the dough, exploring its texture and discussing its smell.

For older children

Older children love to colour and scent their salt dough to make attractive models. Let them use moulds and also work free-style. Try adding spices such as nutmeg and cinnamon to make attractive fridge-magnets for the children to give to their parents at Christmas.

Follow-up activities

* Use other scented materials such as shaving-foam or dry tea in trays for the children to draw and write in.

* Using empty camera film holders, provide about six different pairs of scents and jumble them up for the children to sort and match.

* Have a scented table with a collection of 'smelly' items such as empty plastic shampoo bottles, empty spice containers and so on.

Recipe for salt dough

300g plain flour
1 tbsp oil
300g salt
200mls (approx) of water.
To make – Mix all ingredients together in a large bowl. Bake at Gas Mark 4, 350°F or 180°C. Salt dough is best made the day before you need it. Salt dough keeps indefinitely if kept in a fridge.

Links with home

Ask parents about their favourite smells, and display them on a notice board in 'clouds'.

Cornflour goo

To experience an unusual texture.

Group size

Eight children.

What you need

A water-tray or a bowl, food colouring, water, cornflour, wooden or metal spoons.

Preparation

Pour the cornflour into the bowl or tray and add the water until the mixture is pliable. Add a few drops of your chosen food colouring.

What to do

Introduce the children to the cornflour mixture, encouraging them to feel it and lift it. It will change consistency and dribble through their fingers, providing endless fascination and tactile satisfaction. Some children may not like the feeling and they should be offered spoons to use in the mixture. Let all children experience using spoons as an alternative experience.

Encourage the children to compare the hard feeling of the surface of the cornflour with the slipperiness of the poured material. Cornflour will also squeak as the children move it and dig into it with spoons, and they will enjoy making this noise!

Questions to ask

How did you do that? What happened when you lifted that up? What does it feel like when you do that? What can you hear? When does it change? What else could you do with the cornflour? What did you like doing best?

For younger children

Allow younger children to play freely with the cornflour mixture. Be sensitive about asking them to do more than just enjoying a tactile experience.

For older children

Older children could consider this experience as part of a topic on 'Changes', going on to investigate other materials which solidify, such as plaster of Paris.

Follow-up activities

* Make some blancmange so that the children can see what cornflour is generally used for.
* Make some dribble pictures using Readimix paint in squeezy bottles with fine nozzles (hairdressers are a source of these). Use the same colours as your cornflour mix.
* Try making a thin jelly in the water tray and letting the children explore the feel of that with their fingers!

Links with home

Ask a parent or carer to come into school to make blancmange with the children.

chapter eight

Using large equipment

Children need access to large equipment in order to develop their own strength, mobility and body control by climbing, sliding, pulling and pedalling. Indoors or out, large equipment encourages children to experience movement through all four dimensions and requires space!

Crocodile river

Learning outcome

To move confidently and imaginatively while travelling over and through a piece of climbing and balancing equipment.

Group size
Six children.

What you need
A climbing frame with a platform at the top to act as a boat.

Preparation
Check that the equipment is properly erected and is safe for the number of children who will be using it.

What to do
Suggest to the children that the top platform of the climbing frame is a boat in the middle of a river which has crocodiles in it. Explain that they will be safe on the boat, but they have to keep climbing down to fetch things which they will need and to rescue toys which have fallen into the water.

You might like to act as the crocodile yourself, trying (and failing) to catch children who are rescuing the dolls! The children should choose to drop something into the 'water' to be 'gobbled' up.

Questions to ask
How did you feel when you were rescuing the doll? What did you think was going to happen? What would you have done if the crocodile got you? What did you like doing best? Where was the best place to be? Where was the worst place?

For younger children
Younger children may be upset at the idea of a crocodile catching them, so leave this out. Concentrate instead on the children saving their toys and pretending to swim to retrieve lost essentials.

For older children
Older children could be split into groups of crocodiles and sailors, with several safe 'island' areas marked in chalk on an outdoor play area. The object of the game them becomes to move from island to island without being grabbed by the crocodiles.

Links with home

Take photographs of the children playing and display them with phrases from the Desirable Outcomes explaining what the children have achieved.

Follow-up activities
* Read *The Enormous Crocodile* by Roald Dahl (Picture Puffin) to the children.
* Provide plastic boats, model people and plastic crocodiles or sharks for the water play.

Creepy crawlies

Learning outcome

To develop increasing control and co-ordination using a piece of large equipment to crawl through.

Group size

Four children.

What you need

A tunnel to crawl through (either a purpose-built piece of equipment or a home-made version using small tables put together and covered by a sheet).

Preparation

If possible take the children on a visit to a zoo or to a local pet shop to see snakes and lizards and other crawling creatures.

Ask the children to remove their shoes ready for the main activity.

What to do

Establish the direction the children should travel through the tunnel and the pathway round to the entrance again.

Before they go into the tunnel, practise crawling and creeping around the floor. Remind them of the creatures that they saw at the zoo or the pet shop. Can they pull themselves along just using their arms? Can they move on their backs, pushing with their legs?

Then move to the tunnel and ask the children if they can think of any other ways to travel through the tunnel. Note down any children who show particular strengths or weaknesses.

Questions to ask

What sort of crawling were you copying? Why did you choose to do that? What did you like doing best? What was hard? What was easy? What didn't you like? How did you move your arms and legs? What would you do next time?

For younger children

Encourage younger children to play freely with the tunnel at first, as some do not like enclosed or dark spaces.

For older children

Invite older children to go through the tunnel in a different way each time.

Follow-up activities

∗ Introduce percussion instruments and ask the children to decide which sound matches different movements.
∗ Encourage the children to move supported by four limbs, then three, then two and even one. See how many different combinations of arms and legs the children can use.
∗ Try a 'limbo' style competition to see who can crawl under a cane at the lowest point.
∗ Ask the children to hink about how different animals move. Sing the song 'When I went to the farm' on page 85.

Links with home

Ask the parent of a crawling baby brother or sister to bring the baby in to show the group what crawling is all about!

Pulling a truck

Learning outcome

To show increasing control and awareness of others while using an item of large equipment with wheels.

Group size

Four children.

What you need

A truck or cart suitable for two children to ride in or on, while two others push or pull them. A safe, suitable space.

Preparation

Explain to the children that they will each take a turn at having a ride and at pushing or pulling. Make sure that the children are suitably dressed for physical activity.

It is assumed that this activity will take place outdoors, but it could be organised indoors if you have sufficient space.

What to do

Ask for volunteers to push or pull first, allowing the other children to ride first. Ask the 'passengers' where they would like to go, encouraging the children to use their imaginations about their destination.

Allocate a certain amount of time for being 'passengers' or 'pullers' and ensure that all children get several turns at each role.

Ask the children to feel their heartbeats after they have been both 'passengers' and 'pullers' and talk about what it means when their hearts are beating faster.

Questions to ask

What did you like doing best? What was the most fun? What made your heart beat fast? Why? When was it easy to push? When was it hard? Why? When did you push, and when did you pull? Did you feel hotter when you were pushing or pulling? What would happen if you pushed up a hill? What would happen when you came down?

For younger children

Younger children could try this activity using dolls or soft toys as passengers rather than other children.

For older children

Older children could include this activity as part of their work on a topic such as 'Forces', perhaps seeing how far the passengers would travel with one push.

Follow-up activities

* Using smaller wheeled toys, introduce ramps and slopes for children to investigate the pushes and pulls.
* Devise an obstacle course for prams, trucks and other wheeled toys.
* Look at methods of transporting people which involve pushes and pulls, such as rickshaws, horses and carts and so on.

Links with home

Send a note home with your group saying what you have been doing, and asking parents if they know of any place you could visit which has horses and carts in use.

Taking the weight

Learning outcome

To move confidently and imaginatively taking your own weight on your hands.

Group size
Six children.

What you need
A set of climbing bars, a hanging rope or low trapeze. Safety mats to place beneath.

Preparation
Place your safety mats under your climbing apparatus.

What to do
Ask the children to sit on the floor around the bars or ropes. Encourage them to take turns to see if they can hang from a bar or a rope with just their hands.

Provide adult support to take the weight of any children who cannot hold their own weight and advise them to drop onto the mat, bending their knees as they land.

Once the children can hold their own weight, ask them if they can swing or lift themselves up. Encourage them to stretch their legs, or kick them about or curl them up while still hanging on the rope or bar.

Finally encourage the children to play freely on the equipment, observing them carefully and recording your observations as part of your assessment of each child's physical development.

Questions to ask
What does it feel like when you are hanging from the bar? What else can you do? What sorts of things can acrobats do? Where can you see people swinging from a trapeze? How do your arms feel? What was easy to do? What was really hard?

For younger children
Working with younger children, encourage free play on the bars, ropes and so on and use your judgement when to suggest to the children that they could take their skills further.

For older children
Older children should be able to attempt a somersault over a low trapeze and should have developed enough upper body strength to attempt chin-lifts to the bar.

Follow-up activities
∗ Try to take your own weight on your hands on the floor using bunny-hops, then stretching legs to attempt an early cart-wheel or handstand.
∗ Attempt to hang from the equipment with one hand, or with legs rather than arms.
∗ Develop transfer of weight from hands to feet during climbing.

Links with home

Where children display a particular talent, provide information for parents about dance and gymnastic clubs which operate in your local community.

Sliding down!

Learning outcome

To use a slide to develop control and co-ordination.

Group size

Eight children.

What you need

A slide suitable for use by young children. A safety mat or large cushion for them to land on.

Preparation

Check that the children are wearing clothes which will allow them to slide freely, without any hanging cords or scarves.

What to do

Ask the children if there is anyone who will volunteer to demonstrate what they can do on a slide. Encourage the children to take turns waiting in line for the previous child to finish. Help any child who is unsure, but do not insist if they do not want to. Make sure they see that the other children are enjoying it, and wait until they ask to try it for themselves. Make a note about this for your records.

When all the children have had a turn, ask if anyone can think of a different way to slide down.

The children will usually be full of ideas for different ways of travelling down the slide and will be delighted to demonstrate, but make a note of those who are particularly confident.

Questions to ask

What are you going to do now? How can you do it differently next time? Where were your hands that time? Which way do you think is the most fun? How does the slide feel as you go down it? How could we change this slide to make it even more fun?

For younger children

Free play on the slide is the best approach for young children, since they need time to absorb the experience of sliding. When children start to experiment with different ways of sliding you could intervene and try the main activity above.

For older children

Older children could examine the slide as part of a topic on 'Materials', finding out what slides best and what stops objects from sliding.

Follow-up activities

* Roll toys down the slide and see which slide the furthest.
* Visit the local playground to play on the slide.
* Encourage the children to use large building blocks and planks to make a slide for their toys.

Links with home

Always ask parents for their permission if you want to take the children outside the premises. Consider making a general permission slip for trips as part of your admission form.

See Saw, Margery Daw

To show increasing control and to use large equipment to develop balancing skills.

Group size
Two children at a time.

What you need
A see-saw or sit-on rocker for two children. A copy of the nursery rhyme 'See-saw, Margery Daw'.

Preparation
Make sure the equipment is safe and fit for the purpose.

What to do
Start by singing the rhyme together while sitting on the floor and rocking backwards and forwards in time to it. Encourage the two children to get onto the see-saw or rocker and use it freely. Ask them to tell you how they make the equipment move. Then ask them if they can rock or see-saw in time to the song. Ask the children to swap places and do it again.

Sing some other songs with a strong simple rhythm, such as 'Row, row, row your boat' or 'Bye, Baby Bunting'.

Questions to ask
What are you doing? How are you making that happen? What happens when you go up? What happens when you go down? What would happen if there was only one person? What does it feel like when you go up and down?

For younger children
Encourage younger children to play freely on the equipment, discovering what they can do on it and being given plenty of time for reinforcement. Use your own judgement to decide when the children are ready to do the activity.

For older children
Older children could investigate the properties of a see-saw, experimenting with the placing of the weight in order to balance it out. Give them a problem to solve, such as how to make three equal weights balance.

Follow-up activities
∗ Ask the children to lie on their backs, lift up their arms and legs and see if they can rock backwards and forwards.
∗ Use a rocker-balance to experiment with different items to find out which is heavier.
∗ Some children may be able to sit facing a partner, feet together, join hands and rock backwards and forwards.

Links with home
Send a copy of the words of 'See-saw, Margery Daw' home with the children so that parents can sing it with their children.

On the mat!

To move confidently and imaginatively with increasing co-ordination using gymnastic mats.

Group size
Eight children.

What you need
Padded gymnastic mats of any size (ideally one mat for four children), a clear space in which to move.

Preparation
Check that there is a space of at least a metre all around each mat. Ensure the children are dressed ready for exercise and remove shoes.

What to do
Arrange the children so that each child is sitting in the middle of one of the sides of the mat. Guide the children to where you want them to work if necessary. Start with a warm-up, asking the children to stand up and sit down a few times, jog on the spot and march on the spot.

Then ask them to jump forwards onto their side of the mat, and backwards off it. Do this a few times, then ask them to take turns to jump across the mat and back to their side. Then ask them to crawl, roll, hop and so on in the same way.

Finally ask them to think of other ways of travelling across the mat.

Questions to ask
What is your heart doing now? Why? What different ways did you find to get across the mat? Which was the quickest way? Which took a long time? Why? What did you think you did well? What do you need to practise?

For younger children
Younger children would find the spatial relationship to the edge of the mat very difficult to remember, so give each child their own mat or just concentrate on the different types of movement without a mat.

For older children
Older children can co-operate to develop a sequence which gives each child a turn to demonstrate a way of travelling across the mat.

Follow-up activities
* Use musical instruments to signal different movements on the mats so that a castanet means rolling, a shaken tambourine means jogging and so on.
* Put a mat outside on a grassy area for free play and reinforcement.
* Watch a video of some gymnasts doing floor exercises.

Links with home

Your children may have brothers and sisters who belong to a school or gymnastics club. If so, invite some members of the group to come and demonstrate their skills to your children.

Stop and start

Learning outcome

To show increasing control and awareness of space, themselves and others when using a range of large wheeled equipment.

Group size
Ten children.

What you need

Bikes, scooters, prams and trucks, chalk to make markings on the outside play surface.

Preparation

Draw a roadway on your outside play area. Include some junctions and a roundabout. Write STOP on one of the roads at each junction.

What to do

Before you get the bikes and prams out, take the children outside to talk about the roadway you have drawn.

Position some staff at junctions so that they can remind the children of the need to stop, and what could happen if they don't obey the rules of the road.

Then encourage the children to ride their bikes or push their trucks and prams along the roadway, stopping and starting appropriately.

Questions to ask

What happened when you came to that junction? What could have happened if you hadn't stopped? How do you stop that bike when you want? What would you do if the brakes didn't work? How do you steer that truck? What happens if you don't turn? What else could we have on our roadway?

For younger children

Younger children will be still developing the ability to pedal a bike or push a pram where they want it to go, and this will represent a sufficient challenge.

For older children

Ask older children to design a roadway on paper first, talking it through and testing it with toy cars before copying it onto the outdoor play area with the help of adults.

Follow-up activities

∗ Invite a local crossing patrol supervisor to talk to the children about road safety.
∗ Sing the song 'Hop, hop, stop!' on page 84 and do the actions.
∗ Provide an old bicycle and place it upside-down in your interest corner so that the children can push the pedals to make the wheels go round and then stop them using the brakes.

Links with home

Send a copy of the words of 'Hop, hop, stop!' home with your children so that they can do the actions with their parents.

Step up, step down

Learning outcome

To move confidently, using climbing apparatus with increasing skill.

Group size

Six children.

What you need

A set of stairs (or some large wooden blocks or benches which can be arranged into steps of different heights; five or six steps are enough), the song 'The grand old Duke of York'.

Preparation

Make sure that the steps you intend to use are safe and suitable for the purpose.

What to do

Sing the song with the children first, then ask for volunteers to demonstrate climbing up and down steps. Sing the song again, pausing if necessary while the child gets up to the top and down to the bottom and halfway up, then up and down again.

Let each child have at least one turn, then if there is enough room and you feel it is safe, they could all try to do it together.

Questions to ask

How do your legs feel when you have walked up and down the stairs a few times? What is your heart doing? How do things look when you are up at the top? How do you feel? What does 'grand' mean? When do you climb up and down the stairs at home?

For younger children

Making shallow steps with large bricks is more appropriate for young children, as their legs are often not long enough to step up without using their hands to help them.

For older children

Older children can play games with numbers and steps, where a child calls out a number (up to 6) and the rest of the group have to move to the appropriate step in one stride.

Follow-up activities

* Throw a soft ball up steps and try to catch it when it comes down.
* Make steps using construction toys and sing the song, moving model people appropriately.
* Provide the Duke of York's hat with a large feather for the role-play corner.
* Do the action rhyme 'Christmas' on page 77.

Links with home

Consider having a small notebook for each child which they can take home every evening with a short note of what has been done during the day. Provide a space for parents to write about what has been done at home or any other relevant comments.

Make a circuit

Learning outcome

To show increasing control and co-ordination and an awareness of space, themselves and others. To travel around, under over and through balancing and climbing apparatus.

Group size

Eight to ten children.

What you need

A variety of large gymnastic apparatus, including boxes, benches, stools, tunnels, and mats.

Preparation

Arrange all your equipment into a circuit which will require the children to do different movements, for instance jumping over boxes, stepping onto and off benches, crawling over or under stools, creeping through tunnels and so on. Make sure that the circuit is continuous.

What to do

Explain to the children that you want them to do different movements on the different pieces of apparatus. Ask them to follow each other around in a circle each time.

You should always start a session with a warm-up activity. In this case the children could practise the sorts of movements they could use on the equipment on the floor first so that they can develop confidence to use these movements on the apparatus.

When the children are moving around the circuit, point out each child at some time and ask for a demonstration. Encourage thoughtful and imaginative movements.

Questions to ask

How could you do that again and do it differently? What did you think you did well? What did you find hard? What happened when you got to the end? What did you like doing best? Why? What else can you think of doing? What could we add to the circuit?

For younger children

Younger children are still acquiring the basic skills and it would be much more suitable for them to explore just one type of apparatus at a time in depth.

For older children

Older children can try to make up a sequence of actions on the apparatus to demonstrate to the other children, for them to copy.

Follow-up activities

* Encourage the children to design a circuit of things they would like to do using LEGO or Play People.
* Do some sequenced aerobics to music to start the day.
* Look at other circuits, such as a train track or a roadway.

Links with home

Consider arranging a trip for your group to a local indoor play activity centre. Ask for volunteers to accompany you to improve the adult-to-child ratio for supervision purposes.

Manipulative skills

Name _____

Skills and concepts	Assessment and comments					
	Baseline/1st assessment	Date	2nd assessment	Date	End of year assessment	Date
1. Can make marks using a variety of tools.						
2. Can hold a cup without spilling the contents.						
3. Can build a tower of five bricks.						
4. Can use a knife and fork to eat.						
5. Can draw a recognisable picture of a person.						
6. Can cut with scissors held in one hand.						
7. Can fold a piece of paper into two roughly equal halves.						
8. Can fasten buttons on own clothing.						
9. Can screw and unscrew plastic nuts and bolts in a construction set.						

Learning in the Early Years
Physical Development

Balance and awareness of space

Name _____

Skills and concepts	Assessment and comments					
	Baseline/1st assessment	Date	2nd assessment	Date	End of year assessment	Date
1. Can hop.						
2. Can stand on one leg for a short time.						
3. Can join hands in a circle without adult assistance.						
4. Can walk in a line with others without collision.						
5. Can jump off a low bench.						
6. Can walk along a low wall or bench with adult assistance.						
7. Can jump over an obstacle.						
8. Can find a clear space in which to dance.						
9. Can freeze in position and stay still for a short period of time.						

Co-ordination skills

Name _____

Skills and concepts	Assessment and comments					
	Baseline/1st assessment	Date	2nd assessment	Date	End of year assessment	Date
1. Can thread beads onto a lace.						
2. Can move appropriately during rhymes and finger-plays.						
3. Can fill containers using appropriate tools (spoons, jugs and so on).						
4. Can throw a ball/ beanbag.						
5. Can kick a ball/ beanbag.						
6. Can catch a ball/ beanbag.						
7. Can hit a ball with a bat.						
8. Can skip using a skipping rope.						
9. Can hit a target with a ball/beanbag.						

Gross motor skills

Name _____

Skills and concepts	Assessment and comments					
	Baseline/1st assessment	Date	2nd assessment	Date	End of year assessment	Date
1. Can run.						
2. Can march.						
3. Can skip.						
4. Can travel while jumping.						
5. Can pedal a wheeled vehicle.						
6. Can climb steps or a (short) ladder without assistance.						
7. Can slide down a slide.						
8. Can do a forward roll correctly.						
9. Can demonstrate different ways of moving (crawling, wriggling, rolling and so on).						

Hands and feet

What can you do with your hands?
Rolypoly, rolypoly,
Clap, clap, clap,
Pointy, pointy, pointy, pointy,
Slap, slap, slap.

What can you do with your feet?
Tiptoe, tiptoe, tiptoe, tiptoe,
Jump, jump, jump,
Pointy, pointy, pointy, pointy,
Stamp, stamp, stamp.

Chris Heald

My day out

(A poem about touch)
Small waves that wet my toes,
Warm sun on cheeks and nose,
Itchy swimsuit full of sand,
Slippery seaweed in my hand,
Soft towel to dry my hair,
Rough coconut from the fair!
Sharp stones that cut my knee,
Sticky plaster – Who's brave? Me!

Sue Cowling

Christmas

On Christmas Eve I climb the stairs,
(walk in a circle)
And snuggle down in bed.
(lie down)
I try to stay awake, but Oh!
(yawn)
I'm such a sleepyhead.
(stretch)
I close my eyes and fall asleep
Then wake – it's Christmas day,
And there are presents round the bed,
Hip, hip, hip hooray!
(jump about)

Chris Heald

I saw a slippery, slithery snake

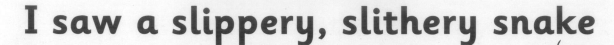

I saw a slippery, slithery snake
Slide through the grasses, making them shake.
Right index finger weaves through fingers of left hand.
He looked at me with his beady eye.
Right index finger and thumb make ring around eye.
'Go away from my pretty green garden,' said I.
Make shooing movements with left hand.
'Ssssssss,' said the slippery, slithery snake,
As he slid through the grasses making them shake.
Repeat first movement.

What are you doing?

What are you doing, little shoe in Green?
I'm going to dance before the Queen.

What are you doing, little shoe in Red?
I'm going to hop and pat my head.

What are you doing, little shoe in Yellow?
I'm going to march with another fellow.

What are you doing, little shoe in Blue?
I'm going to jump like a kangaroo!

Chris Heald

Clay days

Push it, pull it,
poke and pummel;
press your thumb into the ball,
make a mini-tunnel!

Stretch it like elastic,
feel it in your nails;
make a cup, a plate, a car,
make a boat with sails!

Make a candle for a cake
for a special day;
make an apple, m ake a bike
with your piece of clay!

Judith Nicholls

Making bread

Mix up flour,
water, yeast...
Now pull and push and PUNCH!

In the bread tin,
watch it grow...
Then cook it for your LUNCH!

Judith Nicholls

Alphabet actions

(an alphabet action rhyme)

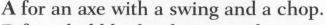

A for an axe with a swing and a chop.
B for a bubble that bursts with a pop.
C for a cushion to snuggle your head.
D for a duvet to cover your bed.
E for an elephant, steady and strong.
F for a fright as you bang on a gong.
G for a goal as you shoot hard and score.
H for a hole that you dig on the shore.
I for an ice-cream that's starting to drip.
J for the juice that you pour out and sip.
K for a king with a crown on his head.
L for a lollipop, sticky and red.
M for a mugful of coffee or tea.
N for a net that you dip in the sea.
O for an orange to peel and eat.
P for a pudding that's steaming and sweet.
Q for a queen eating white bread and honey.
R for a robber who's stealing some money.
S for a snake with a slippery hiss.
T for a target the arrow might miss.
U for umbrella you use in the rain.
V for a van that you drive down the lane.
W for wind as it whispers and moans.
X for an X-ray to look at your bones.
Y for *Yippee!* when your team wins the cup.
Z for a zipper to zip it all up.

Tony Mitton

The mud hole

Harry was playing a brilliant game with his toy animals. He was pretending they were in the jungle. Some of the animals were on the plains (floor), some on the mountains (chairs) and some on the cliffs (table). He was really enjoying himself. Until Mum came in with the vacuum cleaner.

'I've got to clean up now, Harry,' she said. 'You'll have to play out in the garden.'

'Oh Mum, it isn't as much fun in the garden,' Harry groaned.

'Of course it is,' said Mum. 'You've got all the grass and bushes to hide the animals in.'

Harry sighed as he picked up his animals and put them in their box. Scowling, he carried the box of animals outside and sat down on the grass.

'The garden's boring!' he grumbled. There were no mountains out here or cliffs, just loads of grass and a couple of bushes. He took the animals out of his box and put them on the grass. 'You can go here,' he said, moving one of the elephants around a bush.

Splosh! It landed in a muddy puddle.

Harry grinned in delight. Great! Now he had a mud hole for the animals to bathe in. That would be fun.

One by one he took the animals out of the box.

'Swoosh, swoosh!' He waded the crocodile along in the mud. Then he ran his finger along the deep track it made.

Squelch, squelch! He buried the rhino in the mud, right up to its head and wriggled it about.

Splosh, splosh! He stood an elephant in the mud, wriggled it about, then took it out and walked it over a rock, grinning at the footprint trail it left.

Harry picked up some of the mud in his hands, it felt squelchy and soft.

Squidge, squidge! He squeezed it together and rolled it into a ball. Then he put the ball of mud in the middle of the

puddle and flattened the top of it. He stood the zebra on the mud mountain and made it run down into the puddle.

'Splash, splash!' Harry laughed as mud splattered over him. This was fun.

'Harry! What are you doing?' his mother called, coming out into the garden. 'Oh my goodness, what a mess!' she gasped when she saw Harry's mud-covered hands and toys.

'Sorry,' said Harry. 'I didn't mean to make a mess. I was playing.'

Mum sighed. 'Oh well, it'll wash off, I suppose,' she said. 'Now I think you'd better give your toys a bath. But this time you can wear an apron.'

She took an apron and a bowl of soapy water out for Harry to wash his toys.

'You were right, Mum. Playing in the garden is lots better than playing in the house,' Harry told her as he put the animals in the warm soapy water. 'There's no mud in the house!' 'Thank goodness for that!' smiled Mum.

Karen King

Lucy's picture

'My Grandpa's coming to tea today,' said Lucy.

'That's nice,' said Mrs Kelly. 'Now, sit down. We're all going to do some painting.'

'Can I do a picture for Grandpa?' asked Lucy.

'Of course you can,' said Mrs Kelly.

Lucy looked at the big sheet of white paper in front of her.

'Can't you think what to paint, Lucy?' asked Mrs Kelly. 'What would Grandpa like? Something nice and bright? Look at those lovely colours!'

Lucy looked at the red and the yellow and the sky blue paints. 'They're not right,' she said. 'Can I use the glue? Can I stick things on to make a picture?'

'You mean a collage? Of course! But you'll have to sit at another table. There's not enough room here.'

Lucy took her paper to an empty table in the corner. She went and found a pot of glue, some scissors, and the box of scraps.

Lucy loved Mrs Kelly's box of scraps. She liked plunging her hands deep in the box and feeling with her eyes shut.

Lucy started her picture. She cut some soft green velvet into curvy mounds, like hills, and stuck them on the paper. She made a lake out of blue shiny stuff, and put it in between the hills. Then she found some flowery dress material.

'Grandpa has flowers like this in his garden,' Lucy told Mrs Kelly. 'He likes the blue ones best because they have the nicest smell.' She cut round the flowers and stuck them in little clumps along the edge of the lake.

At playtime Lucy was too busy to play. Instead she collected twigs and leaves and then she found two small feathers! She filled her empty juice cup with sand from the sandpit. At last it was time to go inside.

Now Lucy was very excited about Grandpa's picture. She made him a tree out of the twigs and the leaves, and stuck the feathers on the end of a branch. Then she spread some glue in a long winding band over the hills, and scattered sand over the glue to make a path.

'My Grandpa's got a dog,' Lucy told Mrs Kelly. 'She's called Honey because that's what colour she is.'

When Mrs Kelly wasn't looking Lucy cut off a tiny piece of her own hair and stuck it in a shape like a dog lying under the tree.

'That's lovely, Lucy,' said Mrs Kelly, when it was time to stop. She put Lucy's picture safely on the side to dry along with all the paintings.

Lucy couldn't wait until home time. She hadn't seen Grandpa for ages.

Her mum was waiting as usual, but today there was someone with her.

'Grandpa!' Lucy nearly knocked him off his feet.

'I've made you a picture, Grandpa. Look...' Lucy grabbed her blind grandfather's hand and guided it over her picture.

'These are hills, and here's the road...'

Grandpa touched the picture carefully. 'A tree. A bird. And what's this? It feels like your hair, Lucy.'

'That's Honey!' said Lucy, smiling.

'You are clever. And what a lovely surprise. It's the best picture I've ever seen!' said Grandpa.

And hand in hand, Grandpa, and Lucy and her mother walked home for tea.

Nicola Moon

Wiggley Woo

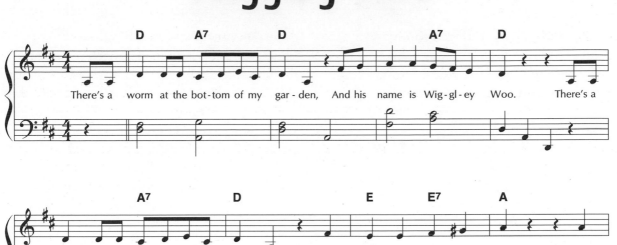

There's a worm at the bot-tom of my gar-den, And his name is Wig-gl-ey Woo. There's a

worm at the bot-tom of my gar-den, And all that he can do is

wig-gle all day and wig-gle all night, The neigh-bours say he's a ter-ri-ble fright. There's a

worm at the bot-tom of my gar-den, And his name is Wig-gl-ey Woo.

Music arranged by Johanne Levy

Hop, hop, stop!

Brightly, staccato throughout

When the mu - sic starts I can hop, hop, hop. Hop, hop, hop. Hop, hop, hop. But when the

mu - sic stops I stop! And when it starts a - gain I hop, hop, hop. Hop, hop, hop.

Hop, hop, hop. But when the mu - sic stops I stop! And when it starts a - gain I hop. STOP!

2. When the music starts
I can skip skip skip,
Skip skip skip, skip skip skip.
But when the music stops I stop!
And when it starts again
I skip skip skip,
Skip skip skip, skip skip skip.
But when the music stops I stop!
And when it starts again I skip.
STOP!

3. When the music starts
I can jump jump jump etc.

Johanne Levy

When I went to the farm

2. I saw a horse go galloping.
3. I saw a hen go strutting.
4. I saw a bird go flying.
5. I saw a lamb go skipping.

Johanne Levy

Heads, shoulders, knees and toes

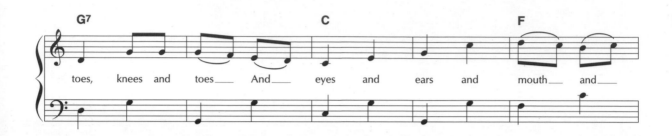

Music arranged by Johanne Levy

Five little speckled frogs

Moderate tempo
Intro

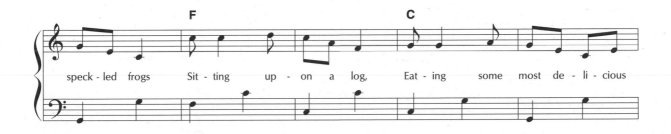

speck-led frogs Sit-ting up-on a log, Eat-ing some most de-li-cious

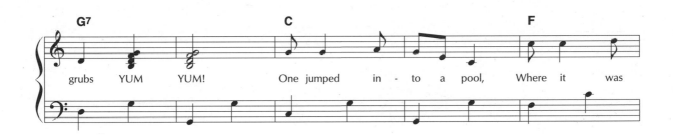

grubs YUM YUM! One jumped in-to a pool, Where it was

nice and cool, Then there were four green speck-led frogs GLUB GLUB!

Music arranged by Johanne Levy

87

Find the pairs

Can you match the shoes up to make pairs?

When you find the pairs, colour them to match.

Matching shoes (P23)

Make a tree

Tearing tissue (P27)

Make a figure

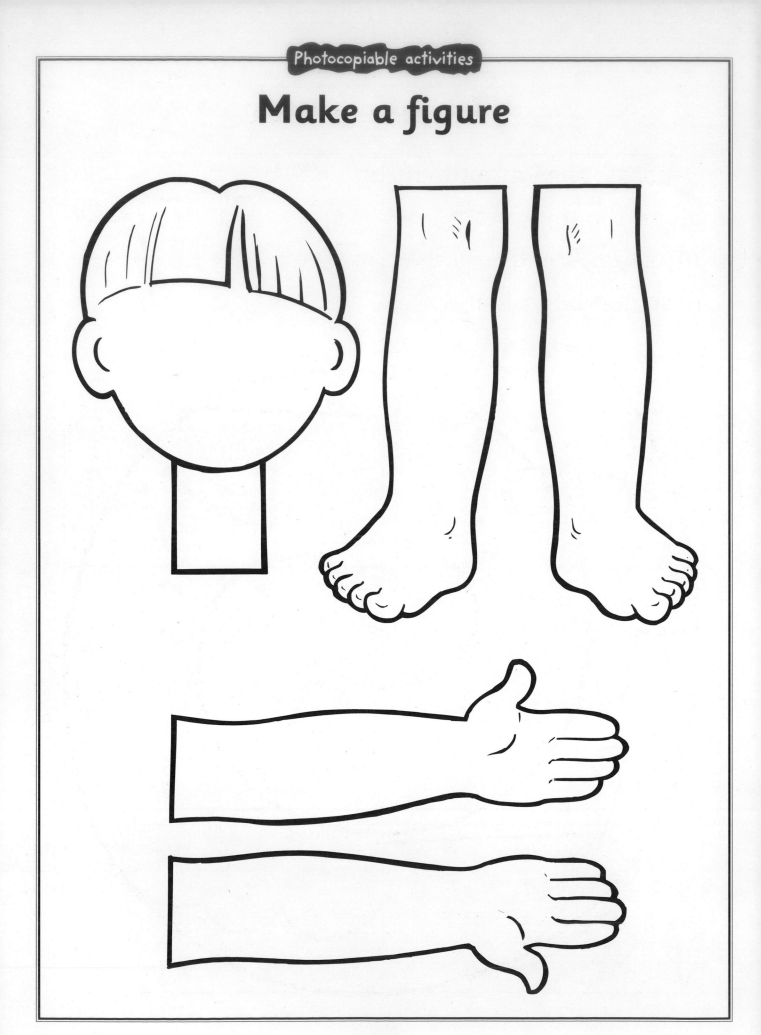

Heads, arms and legs (P32)

Wriggle worm

Decorate the worm then cut
along the thick black lines.
Attach a thread to the worm's
nose and hang him up.

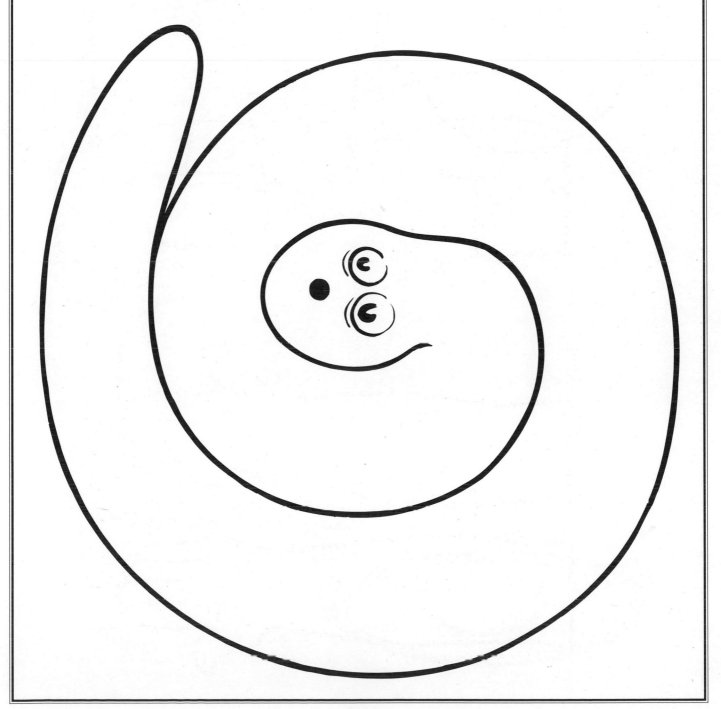

Wriggle through it! (P33)

Ringing bells

Put the bells in order of size.

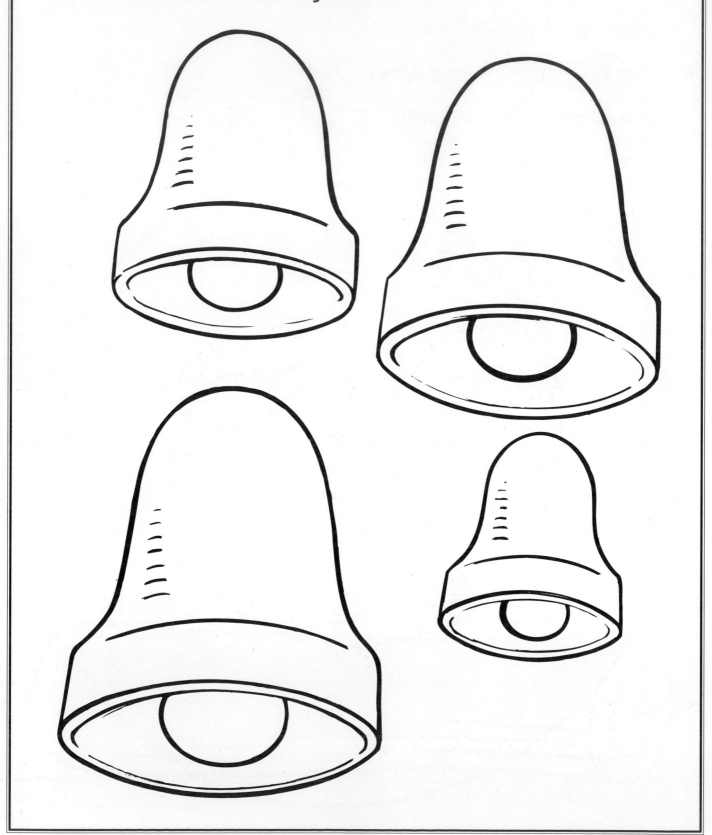

Filling up (P39)

Sitting upon a log

Cut out the frogs and stick them on the log.

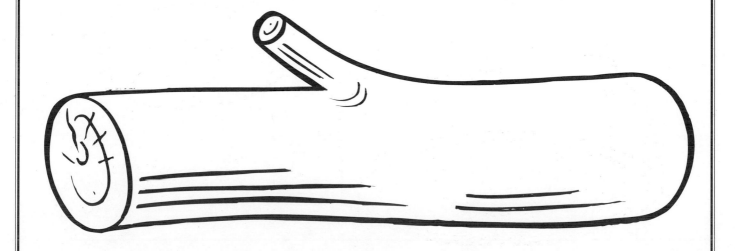

Frog hopping (P43)

Topsy turvy

Some of these things have turned upside-down!
Can you match the things with the upside-down
ones. Draw lines to join them.

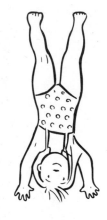

Upside-down! (P47)

Make a crown

The queen of hearts (P56)

Books and videos for adults

Firm Foundations Lesley Abbbott
(Manchester Metropolitan University)

Games for Infants Jim Hall (Leapfrogs)

Children's books

This Little Puffin compiled by Elizabeth
Matterson (Puffin)

How do I put it on? Shigeo Watanabe
(Red Fox)

The Tiny Seed Eric Carle (Picture Puffin)

Ten in the Bed Penny Dale (Walker
Books)

Ten Out of Bed Penny Dale (Walker
Books)

Lili at Ballet Rachel Isadora (Mammoth)

The Slimy Book Babette Cole (Cape)

The Enormous Crocodile Roald Dahl
(Picture Puffin)

The Wide-mouthed Frog Keith Faulkner
(Madcap Books)

Useful addresses

A range of equipment is recommended to
support the activities described in this
book. The items are available from a
variety of sources including high street
outlets, such as the Early Learning Centre
as well as educational suppliers. The
address list below provides details of a
range of relevant suppliers.

ASCO Educational Supplies Ltd
19 Lockwood Way
Parkside Lane
Leeds
LS11 5TH
(0113) 270 7070

NES Arnold Ltd
A division of Novara Group Ltd
Novara House
Excelsior Road
Ashby de la Zouch
Leicestershire
LE65 1NG
(0870) 6000 192

Hope Education
Hyde Buildings
Ashton Road
Hyde
Cheshire
SK14 4SH
(08702) 433 400

EDCO
1 Mallusk Park
Mallusk Road
Newtownabbey
Co Antrim
BT36 4GW
Freephone 0800 243087

Galt-Educational
Johnsonbrook Road
Hyde
Cheshire
SK14 4QT
(08702) 424 477

Early Learning Centre Direct
PO Box 352
Sudbury
Suffolk CO10 6SN
(08705) 352 352

Hands-on
Commotion – solutions for education
Unit 11
Tannery Road
Tonbridge
Kent TN9 1RF
(01732) 773399

GLS Dudley Limited
1 Mollison Avenue
Enfield
EN3 7XQ
020 8805 8333

WESCO
114 Highfields Road
Witham
Essex
CM8 2HH
(01376) 503590

Write to the following address for a
catalogue of other early years teaching
resources, which includes the series'
Learning Through Play and *Themes For
Early Years*:

Customer Services
Scholastic Ltd
Westfield Road
Southam
Leamington Spa
Warwickshire
CV47 0RA
(01926) 816250

The Pre-school Learning Alliance (PLA)
publishes a series of booklets called *Play
Activities*. They are obtainable from:

Pre-school Learning Alliance
Mail order house
45–49 Union road
Croydon
CRO 2XU
020 8684 9542